A CULTURE
WORTH
SAVING

Never too late

ROBERT P. JONES

outskirtspress

DENVER, COLORADO

Outskirts Press, Inc.
http://www.outskirtspress.com

ISBN: 978-1-4327-8308-2

Outskirts Press and the "OP" logo are trademarks belonging to Outskirts Press, Inc.

PRINTED IN THE UNITED STATES OF AMERICA

This book is dedicated to my wife Malinda Usina Jones
who has stood beside me and encouraged me
every moment of life's journey since 1950,
and to Florida's commercial fishing families
whose culture is worth saving.

Thanks to Margo Hall for dedicated editing assistance.

Table of Contents

A Culture Worth Saving   1

Chapter 1 The beginning of conservation
     in Florida   3

Chapter 2 Lumber mill to worldwide shrimping   11

Chapter 3 The Discovery of Florida's Pink Gold   17

Chapter 4 Commercial Fishermen
     in the Greatest Generation   25

Chapter 5 First assignment for Bob Jones   39

Chapter 6 Mighty Rebecca Channel   45

Chapter 7 Naming of the C.O. Jones   59

Chapter 8 Florida Marine Patrol in 1964   63

Chapter 9 The Fish Trap Era   69

Chapter 10 Long line fishing in Florida   77

Chapter 11 The Gulf and South Atlantic Fisheries
     Foundation   83

Chapter 12 The Thompson's of Titusville   91

Chapter 13 Oak Hill   107

Chapter 14 My First fishing experience –
     Mullet Every Way   115

Chapter 15 Florida outdoor writers   121

Chapter 16 Bob Ingle and the St. Petersburg Lab   129

Chapter 17 Senator Randolph Hodges –
     A good man   145

Chapter 18 A Charter Boat Captain   159

Chapter 19 Ralph & Kitty Aylesworth Legacy   175

Chapter 20 "On-Deck" For All Seasons   181
Chapter 21 Holy Mackerel   189
Chapter 22 Fisherman meets Congressman   195
Chapter 23 Riding the River with Rayburn   199
Chapter 24 Florida legislators helped fishermen 211
Chapter 25 The Marine Fisheries Commission   219
Chapter 26 Others who recognized
              the fishing culture   223
Chapter 27 The Tarp Seine Baitfish Net   229
Chapter 28 The shrimp industry's deep roots   233
Chapter 29 One of a kind   237
Chapter 30 Beaver Street Fisheries Mr. Harry 241
Chapter 31 A crystal ball statement
              by Gene Raffield written
              in June 1976   245
Chapter 32 The hiring of Bob Jones   251

A Culture Worth Saving

"If families live their lives in a culture, but disappear without leaving a written record, did they truly exist?"

rp jones -09/30/11

FLORIDA AND FISHING HAVE BEEN SYNONYMOUS SINCE ADMIRAL
PEDRO MENÉNDEZ DE AVILÉS FOUNDED ST. Augustine in 1565.
He brought myriad tradesmen, including net makers and
fishermen who harvested seafood for sustenance and
trade.

From 1880 through 1925, four million Italian immigrants arrived in the United States. Immigrants from
Spain, Portugal, Ireland, Scotland and Scandinavian
countries fled to America. Thousands of families migrated to Florida, searching for economic and political
freedom. Thankfully, many chose commercial fishing.

The culture shock was huge when families that
were speaking diverse languages and observing different
customs met life long Florida natives living in coastal communities from Pensacola to Fernandina. The locals did not
welcome foreign fishermen with open arms. Animosity toward Europeans in 1880 was no different than animosity
toward Vietnamese fishermen fleeing communism in the
1970's or the enmity toward Cuban fishermen fleeing Fidel

A CULTURE WORTH SAVING

Castro's communist dictatorship in the 1980's. America will always be a melting pot where world-wide cultures combine and sometimes collide.

These few recollections are about people who created the Florida commercial fishing culture, a culture worth saving.

CHAPTER 1

The beginning of conservation in Florida

GUY BRADLEY STALKED WALTER SMITH AND HIS TWO SONS THROUGH THICK MOSQUITO-LADEN THICKETS DEEP IN THE FLORIDA EVERGLADES. The Smiths were plume hunters whom Bradley had been trying to apprehend for killing birds in the Everglades rookeries. He found and confronted them at their hunting camp. An argument ensued when Bradley attempted to arrest one of the sons. Gun shots rang out from both sides. When the shooting stopped Bradley was mortally wounded. He bled to death before his body was found the next day, drifting in a boat miles from where he was killed.

Guy Bradley is recognized as Florida's first wildlife officer although he was not always on the right side of the law. In his younger days he killed birds for their plumes but quit when he saw the error of his ways.

After much soul-searching, he joined efforts to stop the slaughter of millions of pink Flamingos, herons and egrets. Killing birds for plumes so feather merchants in New York could decorate ladies hats became unacceptable to Bradley.

After Bradley was killed Walter Smith, the accused

killer, was tried in a Monroe County court. The jury acquitted Smith after testifying he shot Bradley in self defense. Bradley's death and the acquittal of his killer caused citizens to demand something be done to protect Florida's endangered birds.

Intense public outrage forced Florida legislators to address acts of plume hunting, shellfish poaching and other illegal wildlife activity. As a result of Bradley's death and the lack of any statewide conservation laws, the 1913 legislature created the Office of Shellfish Commissioner to which Governor Park Trammell appointed T.R. Hodges.

Florida was a wild state in the early 1900's. Occasionally, Native Americans attacked rural residents. Protecting Florida's coastline and thousands of miles of bays, rivers and creeks was a dangerous challenge which T.R. Hodges willingly accepted.

Most Florida waterways had no navigation aids. Local poachers evaded arrest because they knew every hiding place along creeks and rivers. Nevertheless, Commissioner Hodges relentlessly brought poachers to justice. He did such a good job for conservation that, the 1915, Florida Legislature expanded his duties and authority.

Hodges greatest challenge was crafting law enforcement regulations which the fishermen and hunters would obey. The independent commercial fishermen were not ready to accept change. They didn't believe Hodges would fairly enforce the law. Fishermen knew people with the right political connections were seldom arrested and punished. Hodges never convinced them his law enforcement agents would be any different. In the long run, his harsh enforcement policies cost him his job. When Governor Catts was elected, with strong support from commercial fishermen and dealers all over the state, one of his first actions was to fire Hodges, as he had promised the fishermen during his campaign.

In the early 20th century, hunting, fishing and logging in Florida was unregulated. The commercial fishermen and others who lived off the land and sea didn't want anything from government. It is a trait still important to commercial fishermen who pray to be left alone to catch mullet, redfish, trout, blue crabs, shrimp, oysters and clams in the same manner and same places they have harvested them for over a hundred and fifty years.

Hodges didn't understand commercial fishermen or their culture. Fishing-lore indicates his bias against commercial fishermen was reflected by his harsh manner of law enforcement. These raw-bone, independent fishermen, whose ancestors settled Florida, had self-regulating hunting and fishing laws in their community. The fishermen had their own way of dealing with outlaws. Vigilante law enforcement was sometimes used on out-of-county fishermen. It was simple and harsh.

If, for example, an out-of-county crab fisherman set his gear in local waters, his buoy lines might be cut and his traps destroyed. The out-of-town crabber could either fight the entire community or return home. The smart ones left in their boat. The dumb ones left on their back.

If local fishermen had a problem forcing an outsider to leave, they went squirrel hunting along the shore where the outsider's traps were set. Bullets whizzed close to where the unwanted fisherman was pulling his traps. This type of hunting got the intruder's attention.

In Hodges' time, law enforcement was sporadic, due to the lack of conservation officers. Local constables, sheriffs and judges protected the voting citizens of their community because they kept them in office and on the county payroll. Outsiders were not always judged under the rule of law.

The stubbornness of commercial fishermen to change guaranteed a confrontation with Hodges. The fishermen would not accept law enforcement by a politician in a white uniform who looked down his nose at them and told them how, when and where they could fish. Hodges convinced them by harsh words—and brute force if he had to—that the Florida Legislature commissioned him to enforce the conservation and management laws of the state and he damn well intended to do so.

According to an unpublished manuscript by Robert M. "Bob" Ingle, the first State of Florida marine biologist, "*T.R. Hodges was a fastidious dresser who wore a sparkling white uniform with insignias and badges designating his high rank and the name of his organization. He changed uniforms often when he was in the field enforcing fishing laws. This was possible through delivery of cleaned and pressed uniforms sent by train or horseback from a specific Chinese laundry in Tallahassee.*"

The son of the captain who operated one of Hodges's

gunboats told Ingle that the two one-pound cannons were mounted on the bow of the steamshhip *Roamer*. Hodges used cannons to enforce the law after one of his officers was killed by a fisherman during a confrontation. The cannons protected his agents while they investigated fishing activity in coastal villages and cities up and down the west coast of Florida.

Under protection of the canons, his agents left the safety of the gunboat. On shore they checked the size of oysters, monitored the shellfish harvesting areas and measured fishing nets for proper mesh size and total length. If the nets were illegal they were confiscated, then stacked in a pile on the violators' property and burned. Under his legislative authority, Hodges did not need a warrant. If he suspected an illegal activity had occurred or an illegal net was in a person's possession, he took immediate action without a warrant. Due process was hardly ever considered in this era.

Commercial fishermen are protective of their nets, traps and all fishing gear. I can only imagine the scene in Apalachicola, Carrabelle, Fort Myers or St. Augustine when fishermen and their families gathered around piles of confiscated nets and watched Hodge's agents burn them to ashes. The animosity between the crowd and law enforcement officers was probably brutal. The scowling faces, clenched teeth and crying babies, mixed with raucous shouts from big, strong men in the crowd, was a powder keg. Hodges needed cannons and armed agents to destroy the fishermen's nets. It is amazing Hodges wasn't tarred and feathered.

Hodges received significant publicity from Florida newspapers during his tenure. The following example is from the *New Smyrna News,* published on Sept. 29, 1916.

Hodges Declares Fish Jumped Into His Boat

"The fish are so thick in the East Coast Canal (Intercoastal Waterway) that they jumped into a small skiff towed behind the Seafoam steam craft in which State Fish Commissioner T. R. Hodges came to Miami yesterday, so that official said upon his arrival in Miami. Mr. Hodges arrived in port yesterday, coming from Fort Lauderdale, after making a trip along the entire East Coast. He stated that the Seafoam, drawing three and a half feet of water, easily made the trip down the East Coast Canal.

They are working on the canal at the present time and dredges are taking out the shallow places," said Mr. Hodges. "I am sure that the waterway will be able to accommodate all yachts this winter."

Mr. Hodges was accompanied on the trip by the patrol boat Alice D and two patrolmen. On the way down he saw a man using a big seine. The fisherman dived from his boat and took to the woods while the officials took charge of the seine which is now on board the Seafoam.

Mr. Hodges left Miami early this morning for Boca Raton and Palm Beach, where the Seafoam will be laid up while he goes across the state to Sarasota where he will begin another trip along the west coast. He stated that fish are plentiful along the inland waterways and that never before has he seen such large schools of mullet. On the way down, near Boca Raton, he stated that 18 large mullet jumped into a little skiff being towed behind the yacht and that there are "billions of fish" in the waters of the inside passage. "This will be especially good news for northerners who dislike to go outside but who want to catch fish on the way down," said Mr. Hodges.

The Seafoam is used exclusively on the east coast by the shellfish commissioner while the Roamer, the armed steamer, is used exclusively on the Gulf coast."

Hodges will be remembered for establishing a framework to protect Florida's marine resources. After his career as Shellfish Commissioner, he remained active in Florida politics. He ran for governor in 1924 and 1928 but lost both times. He ran for Secretary of State in 1930 but lost to R.A. Gray.

The Shellfish Commission was replaced in 1933 by tho Florida Board of Conservation, an organization given oversight of the fishing industry by the governor and six members of the Florida Cabinet. The Cabinet system worked properly for decades until the management of Florida marine resources was given to the Marine Fisheries Commission by the legislature, driving a nail in the coffin of seafood industry's harvesting ability. Under a recent Constitutional Revision there is no longer any oversight or appeal process by either the Cabinet or the legislature.

CHAPTER 2

Lumber mill to worldwide shrimping

HARRY F. SAHLMAN BEGAN HIS BUSINESS CAREER IN THE LUMBER BUSINESS NEAR THE TURN OF THE 20TH CENTURY. He cut and sold timbers for construction of fishing boats, houses or anything made from wood. He became a pioneer in the shrimp industry when forced to make a simple business decision.

When America's economy struggled in the 1920's, the price of shrimp at New York's Fulton Market dropped to four cents a pound. The price drop was announced after several Greek fishermen in Fernandina had shipped their shrimp to New York.

Back then a shrimper or shrimp packer didn't know how much he would be paid per pound until the shrimp wore sold. Shrimpers were at the mercy of fishmongers in New York. Unfortunately, not everyone who pretended to be honest and upstanding was.

Shrimp dealers who shipped the shrimp for the Greek fishermen didn't receive enough money to cover the freight much less pay the shrimpers anything. They had no money to pay the bills they owed on several new shrimp boats under construction. They could not pay Harry F. Sahlman for the lumber they bought on credit.

The Greek fishermen offered Sahlman a deal. They

said if he would pay them for their labor and provide the timbers to finish the boats, the vessels would be his and all debts would be settled. He accepted their offer.

That's how Harry F. Sahlman entered the Florida shrimp industry in1928. Over the next four decades his sons, Jack and Donald, and hundreds of loyal employees made Sahlman Seafood the best managed, vertically integrated shrimp business in the world. The big red box known as "Bee Gee" became the gold standard for five-pound-boxes of headless shrimp on the US market.

Derald Pacetti Jr., in his 1980 Master's thesis presented and accepted at Florida State University, described the beginning of the shrimp marketing efforts when he wrote, "Sometime between 1875 and 1877, E. E. Fisher entered the business of preparing and shipping Fernandina shrimp to the New York markets."

Pacetti paints a vivid picture of Fernandina shrimping in the late 1700's and what life was like in coastal Florida. He described how shrimpers boiled river shrimp in brine and sun-dried them to increase the shelf life by several weeks. This simple form of preservation allowed time to ship shrimp by rail and steamboat to New York.

Around 1908, Florida east coast shrimpers used twenty foot open boats with a six horsepower Lathrop or Palmer gasoline engine. The amount of horsepower increased forever when Captain John Santos salvaged a discarded eight-horsepower Vulcan gasoline engine from a sunken menhaden boat.

Captain John rebuilt the engine, made some modifications and mounted it in his little shrimp boat. His bigger engine stimulated other shrimpers to add more power so they could drag bigger nets. Several years later the Vulcan Engine Company increased their engines to twenty-four horsepower and later to thirty-six horsepower giving shrimpers more efficient and profitable harvests. Captain Santos, a native Fernandina fishing innovator, converted his gasoline engine to kerosene which reduced fuel costs considerably.

There's an historical controversy about who actually introduced otter trawls into the United States shrimp fishery. Some writers say it was Captain Billy Corkum who came to Fernandina from Massachusetts. Others write it was a foreign captain delivering goods to Fernandina who demonstrated how North Sea fishermen used otter trawls to harvest bottom fish.

Regardless of who brought the knowledge shrimpers recognized the benefits of having more engine power to pull an otter trawl on the smooth ocean floor. The shrimp fishery greatly expanded as fishermen bought bigger boats to extend their time at sea and find new shrimp grounds.

Local shrimpers wanted to learn where the menhaden fleet caught the large white shrimp when they fished in the ocean. Local shrimpers knew there had to be an offshore shrimp resource waiting to be harvested.

Once fishermen got better engines and larger boats they shrimped farther offshore and began harvesting big white shrimp they always knew were out there. The fishermen monitored their catch records by date, location, average shrimp size and total pounds. From their own logbooks they calculated the movement of the white shrimp from rivers and creeks to areas offshore. This research was validated fifty-years later by a talented and honest biologist who worked for the Florida Board of Conservation. His name was Ed Joyce, a true keeper-of-the-flame.

Because of more powerful engines and better and bigger nets, shrimp production in Fernandina in the early 1900's increased so rapidly that five shrimp canning companies were built on the river. Even with five shrimp canneries working round-the-clock there were still days when tons of river shrimp were dumped overboard because the canneries were at maximum processing capacity. In its heyday Fernandina produced more canned shrimp than any other port in America. This economic boon brought scores of immigrants from all over the world to Florida's east coast.

Many immigrants moved to Fernandina, becoming part of the shrimp and seafood industry. John Ferguson was a Scottish immigrant who lived and loved the American dream. His first job in Fernandina was working as a crewman for a Portuguese boat captain. This eclectic, multi-national language-barrier opportunity is the reason Ferguson spoke Spanish all his life with a wee-bit of a Scottish burr.

He quickly mastered enough Portuguese and Spanish in order to communicate with the captain and crew. He and his wife, Lady Kossie, laid many of the basic building blocks for the US shrimp industry which became a strong and respected segment of the economy. They lived in an era when commercial fishing was respected by consumers and regulators. Captain John Ferguson and Harry F. Sahlman were ethical businessmen whose word was their bond.

There were many others who played a role in building the shrimp industry including Oscar Danberg, a Fernandina African American who built many V type hulls using oak timbers and planking. When Greek boat builders' immigrated to Fernandina later on they built round-bottom boats using pine ribs. The Greeks developed a process of boiling and bending oak ribs into curved hull timbers. Oak is much stronger than pine.

It was common for shrimp boats to run outside the bar in Fernandina, shrimp all day and return before dark with fifty to a hundred bushels of shrimp. Over the years, as more shrimping areas were found to the south, some Fernandina shrimpers moved to St. Augustine because the hundred-mile round trip from Fernandina to St. Augustine was a long trip and the weather in the South Atlantic Ocean can change as fast as the tides.

Moving to St. Augustine meant a shorter run to the shrimp grounds off Cape Canaveral. Shrimpers know white shrimp migrated from the St. Johns River as far as the Cape during their life cycle. There was also an abundance of shrimp migrating from the rivers and creeks in Brevard County.

The Florida shrimp industry was about to experience a huge historical change.

CHAPTER 3

The Discovery of Florida's Pink Gold

THE DETERMINATION AND STUBBORNNESS OF THE SALVADOR FAMILY LED TO THE DISCOVERY OF FLORIDA'S PINK SHRIMP FISHERY. The patriarch, Solecito "Mike" Salvador, has been recognized as a Great Floridian by the State of Florida.

"Mr. Salvador was born in Italy in 1869 and arrived in New Orleans in 1895 on a banana boat. He worked his way to Cedar Key and in 1898 took the train to Fernandina where he became a leader in the shrimp industry. Rigging his boats with modified Otter Trawl nets, he and his brother-in-law, Salvatore Versaggi, expanded their operations to St. Augustine. In 1906, Salvador founded the Salvador Fish Company, using a modified otter trawl to greatly increase the daily shrimp harvest. By 1921, the company was shipping shrimp as far away as Los Angeles, Canada and Denmark. Salvador died in 1924." – Words engraved on his Great Floridian Plaque-

In 1949, pink shrimp (*Paneaus duorarum*) were discovered in the sparkling blue/green waters off Monroe and Collier counties. In a few years the pink shrimp fishery was Florida's most valuable fishery. Unless environmental calamity occurs shrimpers will always be able to harvest pink shrimp from this area.

Salvador was probably the first shrimper to pull a

shrimp net along the smooth near shore ocean bottom off the Florida east coast. In 1902, he steered his small shrimp boat out the St. Mary's River to harvest shrimp off Fernandina Beach, Florida. A few years later Capt. Billy Corkum refined the otter trawl and pushed the Florida shrimp industry forward to its destiny. According to some writers Captain William J. Davis was the first shrimper to venture offshore after the otter trawl was perfected.

The discovery of Florida's pink shrimp fishery began through discussions at Salvador's Fish Market in St. Augustine. Solecito Salvador's two sons, Johnny and Felix, were the main players.

In 1948, while unloading trucks from Key West, Johnny and Felix Salvador often wondered why the plump bellies of fresh red snapper were full of large, pink shrimp. The bright pink color was as unique as the small red dot on the shell. Felix boiled some of the pink shrimp that were still firm and unspoiled inside the snapper's belly. He and Johnny marveled at the sweet taste.

Johnny Salvador, a short, muscular man with thick, black wavy-hair and dark Italian eyes, ran the day to day wholesale operations of the family business. He had wide shoulders, powerful enough to load hundred pound boxes of shrimp on a semi-trailer late at night, for hours at a time, in order to deliver the shrimp to New York on time. He had an easy smile and pleasant disposition. Many of his St. Augustine friends called him "Cat" because of his quiet, stealthy moves.

Felix Salvador knew biology and the fishing trade. He knew that the fishermen who caught red snapper for him submerged the live red snapper in a fish-box filled with slush ice as soon as the hook was removed. The near freezing temperature slowed the digestive process, preserving the pink shrimp in the fish's belly during the trip from Key West to St. Augustine in a refrigerated truck. During the gutting process, Johnny and Felix often found whole pink shrimp inside the snapper's stomach. The Key West red snappers were feeding on pink shrimp when they were hooked.

Other Florida fish houses also found pink shrimp in the red snapper's belly. They yearned to know where the mysterious pink shrimp lived. Knowledgeable shrimpers knew a pink shrimp resource was near Key West, but didn't know where.

Curiosity, determination and hard-headedness got the best of Felix Salvador so he and two crew members took his shrimp boat to Key West to discover the home of the illusive pink shrimp.

Felix was all business when he docked his shrimp boat in Key West. No small talk with locals or partying on Duval Street. Instead he shrimped as hard as he could day after day and kept what he learned to himself. Felix, like his daddy and many shrimpers on Florida's East Coast, had been trawling for shrimp in the daytime for the past fifty years.

Day after day he struggled to locate the pink shrimp, but tow after tow produced nothing. Finally, after trawling in the daytime for two weeks, and just before giving up his quest, he decided to deploy the net one more time at dusk. That drag, at first dark, turned out to be the drag of his lifetime producing the size of a catch fishermen dream about.

After his net was trawling for a few minutes, the big wooden shrimp boat shuddered like it was hung up on something very large, slowing it almost to a standstill. He pulled back the throttle, ran from the wheelhouse to the back deck and began retrieving the net. When the net broke the water, he and the two crew members were shocked and speechless. The net was full of shimmering, live pink shrimp glistening like jewels under the bright lights lighting up the stern. He wondered if he could lift the nets on board without breaking the steel cable. He had never seen so many shrimp in one net in his life. He had never heard anyone bringing in a net so full of shrimp. He and the crew shouted with elation, their joy was beyond description.

Felix Salvador discovered in one history-making drag that pink shrimp burrow during the day and forage for food and migrate at night. The illusive pink shrimp behave exactly opposite from white and brown shrimp harvested off St. Augustine and throughout the southern states.

Felix kept his discovery secret for a short period of time. In a matter of months the economy of Key West would be dramatically improved for the next five decades. It was the hub of Florida's largest shrimp resource. Florida's shrimping industry hit the big-time in 1949, improving thousands of lives and dozens of communities until foreign pond-raised shrimp captured the U.S. market.

White and brown shrimp were the mainstay of

Florida's shrimp industry for 45 years. Nationwide newspapers and radios heralded Salvador's discovery of the pink shrimp resource, declaring that "pink gold" was discovered off Key West. Hundreds of shrimp fishermen throughout the southeast sold their homes and businesses and headed to the Florida Keys.

Unfortunately, many out-of-state shrimpers did not care about conservation in the waters off Florida's coast. They would trawl down highway US 1 if they thought they could catch a boat load of shrimp.

Because millions of pounds of juvenile shrimp were being caught, sometimes illegally, by a handful of vessels, the leaders of the Southeastern Fisheries Association asked for and received help from state and federal scientists to identify the growth cycle and life span of pink shrimp.

The University of Miami and Florida Board of Conservation scientists provided maps showing the life cycle of pink shrimp and the advantages of protecting the juvenile shrimp. A shrimp conservation zone, with no trawling, would achieve maximum pounds and maximum value on a sustainable basis.

After endorsing the biological benefits of conserving the pink shrimp, the leaders of Southeastern Fisheries Association lobbied the Florida legislature to designate 3,000,000 acres as the Tortugas Shrimp Nursery where trawling would never be allowed. This far-sighted decision by the association resulted in establishing the first shrimp conservation zone in the United States, conserving shrimp and their habitat.

This establishment of the Tortugas shrimp nursery was

the fiercest and longest-running battle the association has ever had. It was a major battle the conservation-minded shrimpers and dealers won. The benefit of creating a sustainable Florida pink shrimp fishery in perpetuity is the result of dedicated, conservation-minded members of Southeastern Fisheries Association.

The *St. Augustine Record* published a letter from Felix Salvador in the late 1960s or early 1970s. He was passionate about preserving the St. Johns River, and passionate about preserving the shrimp industry.

The St. Johns Is Our Friend

By Felix Salvador, Chairman
St. Johns River Valley Advisory Committee

To all my friends and enemies of the State of Florida, I submit a true-story which must be told, and remember a word to the wise should be sufficient.

I am a beautiful stream and my name is St. Johns River, the Nile of America in the great State of Florida. I represent all of the rivers, lakes and streams of our beloved land.

Before you came to me I was a beautiful river, flowing peacefully with scenic beauty of trees and lilies, fish and birds, ducks and game which graced my shores, drank my pure fresh water.

Marveled by my beauty, you decided to settle on my shores, to build your factories, to farm the soil, to fish for shrimp, fish, crabs and other seafood's, to hunt my wildlife and kill my birds, to cut the trees in my forest and leave the stumps and limbs to rot and decay.

My story is a simple one, but it's true and what you have done to me will one day be passed on to you.

To those who have settled on my shores: You feed me sewage and filth, soap and detergents, yet I gave you recreation, swimming, fishing and picnic grounds.

To industry: I gave you water to run your mills and trees for your paper, yet you fed me acid, turpentine, sludge and tars, and choked the air from my lungs.

To farmers: I gave you fertile soil to raise your crops so that you may survive, yet in return you gave me pesticides, herbicides and dead animals.

To all my people: I gave my all for in my bosom, I nurtured shrimp, fish, game, and beauty so that they would grow and breed and feed the world, but you destroyed my nurseries and sanctuaries, and when I angered and showed signs of evil you called me names or cursed me.

I call on my Master to send me rain so I can wash the filth from my shores. When you fill my stomach with this filth I vomit with dead fish to give you a sign that I am sick and need your help, yet where are you? Are you looking for another stream to destroy.

Build your factories, feed your families and live and be happy, but remember I can't help you unless you help me.

Build your sewage plant and correct the errors you have caused by negligence. Elect your Water Control Board and Sanitary Commissioners and I'll do my part.

Finally a word to you all who expect so much and give so little: In the end when you are dead and gone I'll still be here just rolling along.

CHAPTER 4

Commercial Fishermen in the Greatest Generation

MEN AND WOMEN OF THE GREATEST GENERATION HELPED BUILD FLORIDA'S SEAFOOD INDUSTRY WHEN THEY RETURNED FROM WORLD WAR II. Some of our heroes serving America with honor and distinction were Sam Cooper of Fort Lauderdale who served in the 716th Tank Battalion that fought the Japanese at Luzon and throughout the Philippines. Bob Starr of Pensacola served on a U.S. Navy light cruiser chasing German submarines and protecting convoys full of men and supplies heading into harm's way. Clyde Richbourg, also of Pensacola, served in the South Pacific fighting Japanese soldiers from island to island. Clyde was a machine gunner participating in fierce hand to hand combat. Jimmy Mc Neil from Indian Pass, Buddy Ward from Apalachicola, Bert Jensen and Larry Shafer from Fort Myers and Jack Hill from Key Largo are a few of the WW II veterans I've had the honor to know and work with during the past five decades.

There are hundreds of Florida seafood industry heroes who served in uniform to protect America. They yearned to be with family and friends. They dreamed to return to the Florida fishing industry.

One of the reasons our veterans are special is they

don't come home expecting praise or undue recognition. They felt they did their job. They believe anyone who loves his or her country would serve if called. Their unselfish service and sacrifices guarantee the continuation of the United States. This chapter is about Paul Herring, a very special American.

One of seven children, Paul was born in Tifton, Georgia in 1920. His wife of over sixty years, Hale Durant Herring, was born in Jacksonville but moved to Darien, Georgia as a young girl and considers herself a full-fledged Georgian.

Paul served with distinction in the Mighty Eighth Air Force during World War II. He was a young warrior assigned to Squadron 339 of the 96th Bombardment Group. He was the pilot of a B-17, commonly known as a Flying Fortress because of its long range ability to defend itself, toughness to withstand heavy damage, complete the mission, then return to base. Paul was in the pilot's seat when his plane was disabled by flak. He knew immediately it was going down. He ordered the crew to bail out. He was the last man out of the burning plane. It was Paul's tenth mission over enemy territory.

He, his co-pilot, Charles Beard of Birmingham, Alabama, and all the crew bailed out and landed safely - though widely scattered - throughout the enemy countryside. When Paul's boots hit the ground he quickly unbuckled his parachute, rolled it up and dashed madly toward a haystack on the edge of a farmer's field. He scooped out enough hay to hide inside while looking in all directions and listening for the sound of German soldiers headed his way. The only sound he heard was his heavy breathing.

The first thing he did was to open his survival kit where he found a neatly folded, silk map of the region. The survival kits were given to each member in the squadron. He quickly determined the direction to Allied lines. He peeked outside, briefly, when he heard a loud explosion not too far from where he landed. Although he didn't see any smoke, he figured the sound was his Flying Fortress exploding when it hit the ground. He cleared a place to lie down and drifted off to sleep from a hard day's work. He did not know what to expect the next morning.

He awoke and looked outside. He saw men and women working in the field. Stepping cautiously from the haystack, he approached the farmers. He asked for water, praying they were allies. Lucky for Paul the entire village was pro-American. They quickly contacted the resistance fighters who arrived out of nowhere and helped Paul evade the German soldiers searching for the plane's crew.

The resistance fighters escorted him, using a circuitous route, to a nearby village where Paul was hidden in cellars, outbuildings and homes. If German soldiers caught anyone hiding an American pilot they were shot on the spot. Through the skill of the resistance fighters Paul evaded capture.

He had a close call when German SS troopers conducted a random search of the houses in a village where he was hiding behind a false wall in the living room. The S.S. troopers searched the house and grounds, but could not find him.

The resistance and local families moved him from one hiding place to another for over six months until he was reunited with the U.S. command.

Paul stays in touch with several of his rescuers. He sadly learned, after the war when he returned from a reunion in England, that one of the families who helped him evade capture was later caught by German soldiers hiding a US pilot. The husband was shot and died, but his wife managed to escape into nearby woods. She eluded the Germans for the rest of the war.

After the war, Paul met Hale Durant on a blind date in early 1947. They were married at St. Andrew's Episcopal Church in Darien, Georgia on July 5, 1947. "Swept me off my feet and love at first sight" comes to Hale's mind when she talks about Paul. They are still very much in love and recently celebrated their 61st wedding anniversary.

Paul and Hale have visited several times with the families who helped him avoid capture by the Germans. The Dutch families visited Fort Myers to reminisce about their special time and place. The powerful spiritual bond between Paul and the magnificent people who helped him survive endures.

After Paul and Hale were married, Hale's father, Alex Durant, brought Paul into the family shrimp business. They lived in Valona, Georgia until 1950 when they moved to Fort Myers where they became leaders in the pink shrimp industry.

Paul managed the boats, crew and shrimp dock workers when they were in Valona. Hale kept the books.

Together they did whatever was necessary to keep their shrimp business profitable.

Paul had difficulty understanding the "Geechie" dialect spoken by many of his Georgia shrimp boat captains and crew. He often asked Hale to translate what the captains were saying so he could settle up their boat accounts.

He enjoyed working with these unique fishermen who preserved a dialect originating from their forbearers who were brought to Georgia from Africa as slaves to work in the cotton and tobacco fields. The slaves were forced to learn English, but maintained as much of their heritage as possible. Their language carried over into the fishing industry although it has mostly disappeared now. Seldom can you hear anyone ask, "Hey mon, you speak Geechie?"

With the discovery of Florida pink shrimp Paul and Hale's lives changed forever. They joined the migration of several hundred shrimp boats and ten to twelve packing houses from Georgia to Fort Myers, Florida.

Shrimping in the early 1950's off the east coast of Georgia and Florida was easier and safer than running fifty miles offshore from Key West to the Tortugas shrimp grounds. Many captains shrimping on the east coast never fished beyond the sight of land. Their shallow draft, under-powered boats were not constructed for heavy weather that quickly springs up in the Florida Keys.

Legend has it several South Carolina shrimp boats

that were headed to Fort Myers were crossing Lake Okeechobee late one afternoon. When the captains lost the sight of land they turned around. They headed back to Carolina even though they saw running lights of shrimp boats in front of them heading to Fort Myers.

Big Lake Okeechobee looked like open sea for fishermen who always shrimped in sight of land. There were no navigation aids or Global Positioning Systems. Some boats didn't have a fathometer.

The east coast shrimpers operated comfortably for years from their home ports using known landmarks such as smokestacks, pine trees and lighthouses to return to their dock in late afternoon or first dark. All of Paul's captains made the trip across Lake Okeechobee with no problems.

Paul's father-in-law, Alex Durant and his partner Sam Lewis, built a shrimp freezer in Fort Myers in 1952. It enabled boats to operate year-round on the west coast of Florida instead of sending them to Texas during the summer season. There were over two-hundred shrimp boats unloading at packing houses on Fort Myers Beach and fifty more unloading at packing houses uptown. The pink shrimp fishery brought millions of dollars of needed revenue to Fort Myers and other coastal cities on the west cost of Florida.

The Durant–Herring Shrimp Co. was formed in 1956. Alex Durant, Paul and Hale Herring bought their first boat, the *Manatee*, in 1959. It was built by Harry Xynides at his boatyard on South Riberia Street in St. Augustine, Florida. Harry Xynides was a master boat builder and a respected member of the St. Augustine community. Legend has it he came to the United States from Greece as a stowaway in the 1930's, but that has never been substantiated.

The *Manatee* was a sixty-foot, wooden-hull shrimp vessel capable of pulling one fifty foot net or two thirty-five foot nets. It was powered by a Caterpillar D 13000, 6 cylinder diesel engine producing one-hundred-ten horsepower. It had a fuel capacity of 1500 gallons. It was state-of-the-art.

Over the years, Harry Xynides built five boats for Durant-Herring. L.C. Ringhaver' Diesel Engine Sales/ DESCO also built five boats including the eighty-foot *Tolomato*. Some shrimp boat owners preferred the six cylinder GM diesel that developed a massive one-hundred-eighty horsepower, but by and large most wanted the big yellow Caterpillar.

The shrimp boats holding compartments weren't insulated in the early1960's because shrimping trips only lasted one or two weeks. It was no problem keeping shrimp fully iced down. The use of sodium bisulphite as part of the ice drip prevented black spots from forming on the shrimp. Some shrimpers still use it.

It was during this time that several Florida boat owners sent their boats to Mexico to harvest pink shrimp along the Yucatan Peninsular. The trip from Fort Myers to Campeche is seven-hundred miles and takes seventy-two hours by slow shrimp boats cruising along at a maximum of ten knots per hour. Most shrimp boats had limited fuel capacity because they historically shrimped close to their home port. To have enough fuel to shrimp the Campeche grounds, they carried dozens of fifty-five gallon drums full of diesel fuel tied down on their back deck.

After the captains loaded tons of ice and drums full of diesel fuel on the deck, there was less than a foot of freeboard as the boats lumbered out to sea from Tampa or Fort Myers to Campeche. There are no reports of any shrimp boats sinking from all the extra weight, but any Coast Guard Safety Officer could have prevented the boats from leaving port.

To save fuel they usually shrimped on the Campeche grounds for at least a month at a time. They shuttled their shrimp on boats headed to Fort Myers or Tampa that had room in their hold. Paul recalls that two of their vessels returned from a Campeche trip with 90,000 pounds of big pink shrimp on board. He said that trip was the largest payday the Durant-Herring Shrimp Company ever had.

There are legendary stories, myths and tales of woe and shenanigans about U.S. shrimpers fishing off Mexico. Captains routinely bartered baskets of shrimp for fresh meat, fresh fruit, vegetables, whiskey and other amenities not normally available on a shrimp trawler. The industry was booming, prices were good, and the Asian shrimp imports were non existent. Virgil Versaggi, an astute Texas shrimp boat owner and industry pioneer once said, "Comarones make a lotta' people rich."

COMMERCIAL FISHERMEN IN THE GREATEST GENERATION

In May of 1952, fifty-five industry leaders gathered in Jacksonville, Florida to create the Southeastern Fisheries Association. Paul Herring served on the first Board of Directors and was an industry leader during his entire career in the shrimp industry.

One of the reasons Southeastern Fisheries Association was created was to protect the recently discovered juvenile pink shrimp off Florida's west coast. The scientific findings by Bob Ingle of the Florida Department of Conservation, scientists from the US Bureau of Commercial Fisheries and Dr. Clare Idyll of the University of Miami all agreed on the biological life cycle of pink shrimp.

The scientific evidence concluded the key for continuation of a sustainable pink shrimp resource was protecting the juveniles. They needed space to mature and migrate offshore to spawn.

Pink shrimp are an annual crop meaning the entire age-class dies within twelve to fifteen months. They can't be saved for future generations. The shrimp habitat must be protected by preserving grasses and keeping the water unpolluted. Pink shrimp have high fecundity. Each mature female shrimp can lay up to 500,000 eggs. As soon as shrimp are visible they become prey for every critter in the ocean. Bob Ingle told me that if every egg survived we would be up to our butts in shrimp.

Most Florida shrimpers wanted a no-trawl zone because mature shrimp are more valuable and the fishery will always be sustainable if juveniles are protected. The opponents of the no-trawl zone wanted to catch the highest number of pounds regardless of size. There was no compromise between the opposing shrimp groups.

Maps showing movement of shrimp in the Tortugas nursery area dominated association meetings and legislative efforts for over two decades. Finally, the Florida legislature established the no-trawl shrimp nursery area. A few years later the federal management council adopted the no-trawl zone in their Gulf of Mexico Shrimp Management Plan.

Paul and all Fort Myers shrimpers strongly supported the no-trawl zone. Most of the shrimp companies, boat owners and fishermen in Tampa, especially Sahlman Seafood, Versaggi Shrimp Corp., Ernie Donini's Superior Seafood, Sammy Fazio and Sam Tringali, supported a nursery area and no-trawl zone. J. Roy Duggan of Georgia and Key West was a fierce proponent for establishing the no-trawl zone.

Several large processing plants, mainly Singleton Shrimp Corporation and Pinellas Seafood Company, were adamantly opposed to a shrimp no-trawl zone. Lou Fischer, Puck O'Neal, Ethridge Morgan and several other packing house owners fought hard against the shrimp nursery. These politically connected shrimp and fish processing companies stalled passage by the Florida legislature for many years, but in the end our tenacity prevailed.

As a result there is a 3,000,000 acre shrimp nursery area off Key West, closed permanently to all trawling. This was a major conservation victory for Southeastern Fisheries Association and the Florida shrimping industry.

Unfortunately the fight was so intense and personal there will always be bad blood between shrimpers who fought to save the pink shrimp resource and shrimpers who opposed the closed nursery area.

Paul was president of Southeastern Fisheries Association in 1976-77. He led efforts which convinced the Florida legislature to grant a sales tax exemption for diesel fuel used by commercial fishing vessels fishing outside Florida waters. The shrimp fishing grounds were located in federal waters and shrimp boat owners felt they should not be forced to pay state tax while fishing in federal waters.

Paul raised over seven thousand dollars from the membership of the association to hire attorney Bob Rhodes, senior partner in the Messer, Rhodes, Vickers and Hart law firm. Through Rhodes efforts and steady lobbying in Tallahassee by Paul Herring, Larry Shafer, Sal and Joe Versaggi, Pete and Jeanette Toomer and many other association members, Florida fishermen were granted a sales tax exemption on diesel fuel while fishing in federal waters. This was an immediate savings of four to six cents a gallon every time a fisherman bought diesel fuel for a commercial fishing vessel. Fishermen received thousands of dollars of extra income due to the work of the association.

Southeastern Fisheries Association spent $10,000 in out-of-pocket expenses and legal fees. After the tax exemption bill was signed into law by the governor, the association's Board of Directors voted to send a letter to owners of shrimp boats fishing in the state showing what the association accomplished and asked for a small donation to help defray the costs.

The Board of Directors didn't expect an influx of donations because there never has been a great desire by fishermen to pay association dues. There is thankfully a hard core of seafood companies who give as well as they take. Many shrimp fishermen don't like to contribute to trade associations. Nevertheless the association mailed the letters asking for any amount of financial contributions.

After patiently waiting for responses and donations for a month, the association didn't collect enough money to pay for the stamps on the letters and the price of a stamp was cheap in those days.

The association created the Tortugas Shrimp Nursery Area and secured a sales tax exemption for the industry. After all this effort, only the few paid for the benefits for all. It's the nature of the beast and always will be.

During Paul's term as Southeastern Fisheries Association's President, Congress passed the Magnuson-Stevens Fishery Conservation and Management Act. It extends U.S. control of formerly international waters out to two-hundred miles.

Florida shrimpers were part of the distant-water fleet along with the tuna and spiny lobster fishermen that opposed extension of federal sovereignty out to 200 miles. Both U.S. Senators - Lawton Chiles and Dick Stone - voted against the extension, but it passed overwhelmingly, led by the Alaska and New England fishing industries.

COMMERCIAL FISHERMEN IN THE GREATEST GENERATION

After the passage of the Magnuson Act all coastal nations of the world extended their ocean boundaries to 200 miles from shore. U.S. fishing boats were banned inside 200 miles of Mexico and this particular loss of historical fishing grounds developed by U.S. shrimpers led to overcapitalization of several fisheries.

Paul and all domestic shrimpers who built Florida's shrimp industry were devastated by the 200-mile extension of federal waters. The industry never rebounded. Not long after that devastating financial blow, foreign pond-raised shrimp flooded the US market, making domestic shrimp a commodity instead of the more valuable seafood item it had always been.

Profits for US shrimpers began a downward spiral to such a degree that in 2009 large domestic shrimp sold for less than a dollar a pound in Louisiana at dockside.

1984 was the turning point for Paul and Hale Herring and their participation in the shrimp business. They attended a World Shrimp Congress meeting in Acapulco, where shrimp farmers, importers and processors gathered to promote their product and announce their goal to capture the US shrimp market.

Paul and Hale listened intently to dire predictions about millions of tons of farm-raised shrimp dominating the United States market within a decade. After considering the monumental changes predicted, they decided to sell their boats. In 1988 Paul and Hale retired from the shrimp industry to enjoy life with friends and family.

CHAPTER 5

First assignment for Bob Jones

IN 1964, MY FIRST WEEK ON THE JOB, I RECEIVED A CALL FROM
SOUTHEASTERN FISHERIES ASSOCIATION PRESIDENT HEBER BELL
WHO ASKED ME TO DRIVE TO ST. PETERSBURG FOR A MEETING. He
suggested I begin my trip in Pensacola, stopping along
the way to introduce myself to members on the west
coast listed in the membership booklet. He asked that I
leave on Tuesday for Pensacola and plan to arrive at his
home on Saturday to spend the weekend with him, his
wife Doris and Shag, their feisty Schnauzer. He said we
would be going to the Don CeSar Hotel on St. Petersburg
Beach to meet Seton Thompson and Jack Brawner at the
Bureau of Commercial Fisheries office to discuss seafood
marketing. From this first meeting with Seton and Jack,
Heber became known as the "Father of Florida Seafood
Marketing" and led seafood marketing efforts from 1965
until his death. Robert Bell, Heber's youngest son, still
participates in the industry and presents the Heber Bell
Award for integrity at the association's annual meeting.

I'm a person who believes my Higher Power has a
plan for me. How fortunate it was for me that the first
name on my list to visit was American Seafood Company,
owned and operated by Clyde and Loretta Richbourg.
There were no cell phones or fax machines or GPS. All I

had was a road map showing how to get to the water-front, turn right on Palafox Street and go west to the foot of "B" Street where the members were located. When I approached "B" Street I recognized shrimp boats tied up along the docks and saw a giant American flag painted on the two-story white, concrete block wall of American Seafood.

As a 30 year old I felt I could conquer the world, but there was still anxiety as I parked the car, got my brief-case and walked up the stairs to the loading platform. I asked the first person I saw if Mr. Richbourg was around. The young man in white rubber boots who was loading shrimp boxes smiled and said, "Mr. Richbourg is in the office."

I had my good black shoes on – probably my only pair of good shoes – that quickly sucked up shrimp juice that was on the floor. This was a good lesson to learn as the smell of shrimp stayed with me for at least four days. When I walked into restaurants on the trip south I felt the other patrons smelled me before they saw me. Maybe not.

Heber Bell emphasized in his phone call that members are usually very busy running their business and did not have time to shoot the bull. He said to make my visits quick, answer their questions and let them get back to business. That has been my style since 1964.

Clyde Richbourg was a big man. He was big in size, big in heart and big in personality. I learned years later how big he was in his service to America. He served as a 50-caliber machine gunner throughout World War II in the Pacific. Like all men from the Greatest Generation he never said much about his service, but did tell me several gripping experiences he had that have stuck with me all my life. He truly saw the gates of hell in many fierce battles. He felt lucky to make it back to Pensacola.

I was wearing gray pants, white shirt, red tie and a blue sport coat. In a working fish house, my attire was as out of place as tennis shoes at a church wedding

Clyde rose from his chair as I walked into the office, shook my hand, looked into my eyes and welcomed me to Pensacola and my new job. He introduced his wife Loretta, a black-haired beauty who was smiling and seemed glad to meet me. He asked me to have a seat and we proceeded to become acquainted.

Thinking back I wonder what Clyde and Loretta thought about a young whippersnapper who knew nothing about their business or the nuances of the seafood industry taking over the formidable job of running Southeastern Fisheries Association. They made my first foray into the Florida commercial fishing culture very pleasant.

My arrival coincided with lunchtime so they had fried shrimp lunches delivered that were absolutely delicious. Loretta said American Seafood supplied the shrimp and knew the fry cook would not overcook the fresh brown shrimp. I learned later that Loretta had owned a restaurant and knew the food trade quite well.

We visited for an hour which I thought was pushing my welcome. Clyde made a few calls then told me Francis Taylor, Joe Patti and Allen Williams wanted me to drop by and introduce myself, which I did. I felt Pensacola was a big happy family and thinking how great that was for everyone. If naivety is measured by pounds, I topped the scales at a thousand pounds. I had no idea about the ferocious competition existing in the Florida seafood industry. It didn't take long for me to hear one person say something bad about another person, expressing anger because they lost a boat to a competing fish house. One thing I knew long before I went to work with the association was never carry tales.

Francis Taylor was a past president of the National Fisheries Institute and was a wealth of information about the history of the fishing industry not only in Pensacola, but many places in the world. We went to lunch the next day at the Pensacola Yacht Club. It reeked of old money, the smell of whiskey and was a place where Pensacola politics abound.

Allen Williams, one of the big four seafood dealers in Pensacola, was an energetic man doing five things at once. He told me about the problems with the Baylen Street Bandits selling shrimp from their boats directly to the consumers and felt strongly they should undergo the same kind of health inspection he goes through every month.

Joe Patti, one of the biggest and most successful seafood dealers in the southeast, was already known to me because of family connections who bought all their seafood from Joe Patti and Sons. Captain Joe, when I met him, was a short, powerfully built fisherman, fish dealer and all round entrepreneur who worked from dawn to dusk every day taking care of business. His son Frankie was working in the plant that day. I talked to him for a few minutes, but this was a fish house where I needed to get in and get out. The Patti's had numerous jobs to perform and did not have time for small talk. It was not unfriendly, but quite evident more important things needed doing than talking to a young man who might not know enough to find his way out of the building.

A novel could be written about Joe Patti and family and how he achieved the American dream by working long enough and hard enough for the financial rewards to follow. Captain Joe Patti was instrumental in helping many people succeed in the seafood business including Steve Cox of Tampa and Bob Starr of Pensacola. There are awesome stories that should be written someday.

I didn't meet Captain Sidney Clopton and his family on this first trip, but did on my second visit. Clyde and Loretta spoke highly of Johnny, Jeff and especially Captain Sidney whose shrimp boat was named *The Ten Kids.*

My first experience with the Apalachicola oyster industry occurred the next day. Cecil Varnes, Duddy Ward, Jimmy Mc Neil and Jesse Kirvin were the main supporters of the association. The seafood industry was the engine for Franklin County's economy. That was so in 1964, still is and always will be. I spent the day meeting local officials and ate a great shrimp and mullet lunch at The Grille. The trials and tribulations of the oyster industry are not much different today than back then except state and federal regulations have increased tenfold.

I drove to Cedar Key the next day to call on Past SFA President R.B. Davis. R.B. was a respected leader in the Florida seafood industry all his life. He was one of the best friends Randolph Hodges ever had and vice versa. After Cedar Key I visited a crab plant in Crystal River, but do not recall if it was owned by Peter and Roger Newton's family or not. I do remember seeing more crab meat being packed in one building than I had ever seen in my life. I would have been content to find a fork and sample a pound or two of the big lump meat if the opportunity had presented itself.

CHAPTER 6

Mighty Rebecca Channel

PETE AND JEANETTE TOOMER WERE STANDING ON BOARD THEIR SHRIMP BOAT *EASY RIDER*, ANXIOUSLY WAITING FOR US AT THE A & B LOBSTER HOUSE DOCK. They had filled large coolers with Cuban sandwiches, eggs, sausages, milk, cold drinks, bacon and coffee for Florida legislators going on the annual shrimping trip to Fort Jefferson National Park. The legislators arrived at the dock in Florida Marine Patrol automobiles and began stowing their gear. They were tired after the long flight from Tallahassee in privately owned airplanes and keen to set out to sea on a commercial shrimp boat.

There were four comfortable sleeping bunks on the shrimp boat so Senator Dempsey Barron, the Dean of the Senate, got first pick; then, three legislators with the most seniority got the other soft bunks. Everyone else got a clean, thin mattress to lay on wherever they found an open spot on the deck or roof.

The running time to Fort Jefferson, including slowing down to trawl for an hour, usually takes ten hours. The *Easy Rider* was spick and span. It was freshly painted for the legislative trip and recently inspected from stem to stern by a marine surveyor. The powerful 343-Caterpillar-diesel-engine generated sufficient power to push the heavy boat at a top-speed of 10 knots. The 343-Cat is very dependable in all kind of weather.

If unpredictable winds were howling in Rebecca Channel the trip could take twelve or more hours. On that night Rebecca was at peace. The night was crystal clear, slightly cool for May with a sky full of stars and constellations easily identifiable. The sea was less than 4-feet, gently pushed by a 12-knot easterly wind.

Captain Pete steered the boat out the Key West Harbor with Mallory Square on his port side. He rounded Tank Island then picked up the Northwest Channel. As we headed out to open sea, Captain Pete told the legislators and guests that the stilt house on his port side was thought to have belonged to Ernest Hemingway.

He proceeded cautiously because the submerged East Jetty and the West Jetty have sunk many boats. After passing the Northwest Channel sea buoy, he put the *Easy Rider* on a northwest course keeping Smith-Shoal-Light off the starboard side until he reached seventy feet of water.

After running for a couple of hours after dark, but before setting the two large shrimp trawls, he deployed a small try-net for fifteen minutes. When he pulled the try-net back on board it had caught several pounds of pink shrimp. He examined them carefully and knew the shrimp harvesting demonstration that followed would be a memorable and tasty experience for the legislators.

He set the shrimp nets overboard in seventy feet of water then headed due west. After the nets were on the bottom everyone tried to get a couple hours rest. Most were too excited to sleep.

Five legislators were stretched out on the vessel's roof, five were on the back-deck and four senior leaders dozed in the soft, warm bunks inside the cabin.

A few hardy legislators and all the industry hosts sat around the back deck exchanging war stories and discussing how the world was going to hell in a hand basket.

Captain Hersey, a slight-built wisp of a man who has shrimped since he was a teenager, was in the wheel-house to assist Captain Pete in case of trouble. Captain Pete eased the throttle forward and maintained a speed of three knots as the net slid smoothly over the flat ocean floor.

After two hours, it was time to retrieve the big net. Captain Pete flicked the switch on the console, illuminating the entire back deck. At the same time Captain Jack engaged the powerful Stroudsburg winch to wind in the net. Within three minutes every legislator was awake, intently watching the net retrieval process. They heard the steady groan of the winch and watched strong steel cable fill the steel drum as if it was monofilament fishing line being wound up on a Garcia reel.

The wooden shrimp doors used to keep the net open during trawling broke the surface then slid along the top of the dark water creating vivid phosphorus trails as the vessel idled forward. Cameras flashed as most of the legislators had never seen a shrimp boat retrieve its nets. They were amazed when Captain Hersey gently set the heavy doors into their storage racks on the back deck.

The lazy-line, trailing in the water alongside the net, was hooked with a long-handled gaff to swing the net over the back deck. As soon as the nets were retrieved and stopped swinging back and forth like a pendulum, the cod-end rope, tying the bottom of the net shut, was loosened. A cornucopia of sea life spewed forth wriggling, popping and swishing all over the back deck and in-between the feet of legislators who wanted a closer look at the harvest.

There was a shout of "good job" from the legislators. They were witnessing, for the first time, the many forms of marine life brought from the ocean and released on the back deck of the *Easy Rider.* This was truly a sight they will never forget.

After the net was emptied, it was put overboard and pulled along the surface to rinse it out. Legislators had scrambled down from the roof and waded among the multitude of pink shrimp, fish, spider crabs and bottom detritus. They snapped pictures to show family and friends how they harvested Key West pink shrimp.

Pete and I began culling shrimp into small piles and popping their heads off, using both hands. We tossed the headless shrimp into wire-mesh baskets. Everything else was shoved overboard through the scuppers offering a feast to the critters following the *Easy Rider.* The by-catch from a short tow was mostly alive as it hit the water, but sharks, king mackerel, bonito and other predators following the shrimp boat consumed the fresh sea life. Very little by-catch ever reaches the bottom in deep water and nothing stays on the bottom very long.

Senator Dempsey Barron and Representatives Jim Tillman, Gus Craig and Dick Renick pitched in immediately, helping to head the shrimp. Senator Barron, from Panama City, was one of the commercial fishing industry's most ardent supporters throughout his entire legislative career. He was a rancher and entrepreneur, raw bone and tough as anyone I have ever met.

Representative Gus Craig represented St. Augustine and was my mentor. He served in the Army Air Corps and flew numerous missions during the Murmansk Run, Russia's link to the Allies, during WW II. It was also the port to which the United States delivered millions of ton of goods. Gus stood-up proud for the fishing industry throughout his long life.

Jim Tillman was a rough, tough cattle man used to working with his hands and super-strong back. He was the Minority leader at a time when there were only a few Republicans in the Florida legislature. He was "old school" and his word was always his bond.

Dick Renick was a Miami boy with a heart of gold and a willingness to learn anything new. He was a strong Democrat with strong feelings for the working man. His laugh and sense of humor were world-class. He was a friend of the fishing industry as was most of the Miami delegation including House Speaker Dick Pettigrew. These "legislative shrimp-headers" filled three baskets of shrimp in record time and received a raucous round of applause and comments from their fellow legislators.

Representative Jerry Melvin from Okaloosa County, another friend making his first offshore trip, asked if we were going to eat all the shrimp we had caught. Captain Pete told him we'd eat every one of them as well as grouper, lobster and snapper they would catch the next day.

After showing the legislators how pink shrimp are harvested and after answering questions, he increased the speed and passed north of Ellis Rock, New Ground and Rebecca Light. After clearing Rebecca Light, he headed southwesterly keeping Pulaski Light on his starboard side until he got the Pulaski Light lined up with the fort's lighthouse. At that point he headed westerly keeping the two lights lined up all the way to the Red Stake which is the east entrance to Fort Jefferson.

We sighted Fort Jefferson at dawn. The chilly legislators, who slept all over the roof and deck rolled up in blankets looking like a sarcophagus convention, eased off their mattresses. They got their sea legs and headed to the wheelhouse in search of the smell of strong coffee and hot, buttered Cuban bread loaded with thick slices of ham, roast beef and bologna. This is not a common Tallahassee breakfast, but not much was left over after they got their fill.

The legislators grabbed a cup of coffee and bread to dunk in it, then lined up along both sides of the boat gazing at the huge brick and concrete structure rising from the sea. It was hard to believe they were seventy miles from the mainland. Birds flew around the shrimp boat, squawking and begging for any morsel of food. Legislators obliged them by tossing pieces of bread into the air that were caught before a crumb hit the water.

We tied the *Easy Rider* to the sturdy Fort Jefferson dock. Everyone grabbed their gear and followed the Park Ranger to their sleeping room inside the Fort. We rented cots for $1.00 per night, but the ancient kitchen with a large brick oven was made available for free. We carried the groceries, including the shrimp, to the kitchen and began preparing for lunch. It seemed I was always in the kitchen cooking fish, lobsters, grits, collard greens and tons of biscuits that we ate with butter and special home-made cane syrup one of the North Florida legislators brought along for the trip.

The legislators snorkeled in the moat or shallow water near the fort and fished for tarpon off the dock all day Saturday. There were a couple of bikes so several legislators rode around the entire Fort. They took time to visit where Dr. Mudd was imprisoned after treating John Wilkes Booth. Everyone admired the brick work of true craftsmen who built fancy arches and patterns not seen very often.

After a supper of the finest and freshest seafood in the world, some of us played low-stakes poker. Others did more sightseeing and later discussed the Florida seafood industry and where it was heading.

Representative Jim Tillman and I walked down to the dock, talking about fishing and life in general. We were sitting on a bench looking at the shrimp boat when Captain Pete eased over and told us a cold front was coming through tonight and the trip back to Key West was going to be unpleasant.

He asked if I could postpone the trip back until the

weather got a little better on Monday. I told him we couldn't delay our return to Key West because the leaders of the legislature were with us and they had to be in session on Monday morning. We had to get all of them safely back to Tallahassee Sunday night or early Monday, in time for the session. I asked Pete if we were in any danger making the crossing through Rebecca Channel. He said the *Easy Rider* could stand it if the legislators could stand it. I told him we had no choice.

Pete looked at me for a long moment, smiled, chomped down on his Optimo cigar then said "okay." He turned and headed back to the shrimp boat to lash down everything on the deck and to check the metal planers on the ends of the outriggers, hoping they could be used to stabilize the boat if possible.

It was about midnight when I thought a Banshee had come among us. There was no glass in the windows where we slept so cold winds howled throughout the cavernous Fort all night. Shortly after the wind arrived, the skies opened up and the torrential rain began. That was one of the few times, other than being in a few hurricanes, I felt the sting of rain coming at me sideways. Everybody hunkered down inside the fort to find a spot out of the wind and rain then tried to go back to sleep. The rain fell for the next five hours.

We all awoke on Sunday morning to a mean-looking sky. Dark, gray, fast-moving-clouds was all we could see. The twenty-degree temperature drop made us shiver like we were inside an ice plant. Nobody brought heavy coats and there were only four rain-slickers on board the

Easy Rider. Most of the legislators wore shorts or light khaki pants and t-shirts. I worried what the trip back to Key West would be like.

We delayed departure until 8:00 AM praying the wind would die down. It didn't and we had to get the legislators back to Tallahassee. Crunch time came.

Pete and I helped everyone get their gear on the boat. I was apprehensive knowing we had the leaders of the Florida legislature on an isolated, federally-owned island, 70-miles from Key West. It was our responsibility to get them home safely.

We gathered everyone on the dock. I told them it was going to be a rough trip, but assured them the *Easy Rider* was well-built and that Captain Pete and Captain Hersey had weathered rougher conditions all over the Gulf of Mexico on many occasions. After everyone was accounted for, I climbed on board making sure everyone had a life preserver. I saw anxiety on their faces. We had legislators from all walks of life including WW II veterans, businessmen, lawyers, doctors and farmers. They all had families and held important positions in the Florida legislature.

It was quiet inside the wheelhouse as we left the protection of the fort. Everyone morphed into private thoughts as the fierce wind whipped up white caps as far as the eye could see. Looking at the horizon, I noticed "huge buffalo herds stampeding, fast and furious." I knew we would be in ten to twenty foot seas in Rebecca Channel. I remembered from previous crossings that the waves come from all directions and the time sequences between the waves are totally variable. This motion feels like you are in an old-fashioned washing machine.

Everything was stowed or securely tied down to prevent injury when the rock-and-roll party began. Twenty men crammed into the wheelhouse, galley and bunk area. When we reached the heavy seas, the face on one of the Cabinet aides turned a pale shade of green. His breakfast immediately speckled his shirt, pants and shoes and the dark gray galley floor. The overpowering stench launched a cacophony of ugly, queasy sounds from several other legislators standing in the wheelhouse.

When the heaving began, I quickly stepped outside and grabbed hold of a guy wire running between the gunnels and roof with my right hand, then grabbed the handle of the wheelhouse door with my left. I stood facing the wind to let the salty waves kill the very recognizable pungent odor.

A few minutes later Representative Jim Tillman went to the port side of the boat and assumed the same stance I was in. We glanced at each other and smiled knowing we were about to take one hell of a ride across Rebecca Channel.

Trying to maintain balance in the pouring rain and a howling wind, I thought about the responsibility Captain Pete and I had to bring these good men home. If something happened to the *Easy Rider* there was a good chance the brain trust of the Florida Legislature and the rest of us would drown. I thought about my wife Malinda and our five children.

The realization that the roughest seas were dead

ahead and there was nothing I could do to change my situation played weird scenarios in my head. I wondered what in the hell I was doing on a small, round-bottom-wooden shrimp boat, seventy miles from shore, at night, in a vicious squall in the Mighty Rebecca Channel, a channel that's probably claimed vessels since the 1500's. The situation was surreal.

The winds screamed when we entered Rebecca Channel. The first navigation light would be Loggerhead Light, a great distance away. When we passed Loggerhead we would use the same markers we passed on our way to the fort. That was our plan.

Captain Pete radioed Lt. Ed Little at the Florida Marine Patrol office in Key West and told him we were leaving Fort Jefferson and he said he would call when he saw the Smith Shoal light so they could determine our estimated arrival time. He softly placed the microphone back in its holder and once again became totally focused on keeping the shrimp boat headed directly into the waves as much as possible while trying to stay on course. Talking was over. It was time to hunker down for a shrimp boat ride of a lifetime.

I felt the waves quicken and the wind strengthen as we plowed through the angry sea. Just when I thought we'd be trapped in the trough in front of a high wave, the boat popped up like a cork with the big Caterpillar 343 running smooth as a clock, pushing strong and steady towards the next encounter. Every once in a while Captain Pete flicked on the spotlight to see what was ahead then flicked it off quickly because all he saw were immense waves bearing down on the *Easy Rider.*

I knew crossing Rebecca Channel would be the big-gest challenge and I was mentally ready. When the worst part of the night began after standing outside the wheelhouse for several hours, I felt a surge of strength throughout my body. Gripping the wire tightly for several more hours caused no strain whatsoever.

I felt safe on Pete's well-maintained shrimp boat. Having two captains at the helm with twenty-five years experience was great, but I still said enough Our Father's and Hail Mary's to gain a plenary indulgence.

I knew we were fine even before the sea calmed a little when we broke loose from Rebecca's grip. Laughter and loud talking began. Representative Jim Tillman and I finally came inside to sit down for a moment. We began cleaning and mopping the wheelhouse which smelled like a drunk-tank on Saturday night in Orlando.

Captain Pete pulled a dry Optima cigar from his shirt pocket, bit the end off, spit the tip on the floor, then put the fat cigar between his teeth and grinned like a first-time daddy in a maternity ward. Everyone clapped and Captain Pete and Captain Hersey smiled to acknowledge their congratulations.

We unloaded the legislators at the dock by the A & B Lobster House, shook hands and told each other we would never forget the trip to Fort Jefferson. The waiting Marine Patrol officers transported the legislators to the airport. They got back to Tallahassee in time to shower, get a little sleep, and make it to the legislative chambers on time. The conversations they had with the legislators who didn't make the trip must have been very interesting.

I spent another day in Key West helping Captain Pete and Jeanette clean up and relaxing on the patio of their waterfront home. We knew we had been lucky, but knew fishing skills honed over many decades is the best insurance against high winds and ugly seas when the unexpected happens, especially in Rebecca Channel.

The annual legislative trip to Fort Jefferson continued for several more years until rules supported by misguided lobbying efforts banned forever the ability to take legislators on an educational shrimping trip. Southeastern Fisheries Association would never have been able to establish the Tortugas Shrimp Nursery Area without making those shrimping trips to the Dry Tortugas, showing the legislative leaders exactly what we wanted to preserve.

CHAPTER 7

Naming of the C.O. Jones

THE DESOLATE STRETCH OF US 1 HIGHWAY FROM HOMESTEAD TO KEY LARGO IS FRAMED BY PRISTINE WATER OF ALL SHADES OF GREEN AND BLUE. The view can be mesmerizing. Glancing at lush green mangroves with roots intertwined in mind-boggling geometric patterns and the spectacle of sea birds working the shallow water for a morsel of food makes concentrating on driving difficult, especially on this segment of a two-lane road that has claimed so many innocent lives.

The overpowering smell of seaweed, detritus and native flora kept my nostrils in the full open position. This narrow stretch of asphalt highway becomes a race track for macho-men and drunk-drivers late at night. Speeding through paradise like a maniac on the way to hell is an oxymoron.

I was on my first ever trip to the home of the Conch Republic. The company car was a dark blue 1960 Chevrolet Impala. It was like a new car to me after driving my 1957 Volkswagen bus for the past four years on trips which included Florida to Oklahoma and back several times. The odometer had stopped when it reached 175,000, a few years back.

Edwin Felton was a true Key West Conch. He was big, burly and loud-talking when he was upset. He had a military style crew cut, but he had never served in the military. His sense of humor was well known throughout the fishing industry. He was the kind of man you shook hands with to seal a deal.

He would send 20,000 pounds of spiny lobster to your plant without a signed contract if he trusted you. His wife Marci was quieter than Edwin, but had a wit and sense of humor that cut to the bone.

Edwin and Marci had invited me to spend a few nights with them to learn about the spiny lobster industry, an invitation I gladly accepted. Their home was in the old part of Key West where streets are rough-paved and Key lime, guava, palm and banyan trees nestled next to giant bougainvillea, Birds of Paradise and simple yellow and white flowers that seemed always to be in full bloom. The Felton's home was near the home where my mother had lived when she was young. Her daddy was an engineer on one of Henry Flagler's trains running from Key West to Miami.

The Felton's house had faded yellow and brown coquina walls. Its massive, hand-poured concrete foundation had withstood every hurricane since it was built in the 1930's. It had three or four bedrooms, a living room and large kitchen area. I ate pan-fried spiny lobsters his boats had caught the day before, served with fresh avocadoes grown in their backyard. The Felton's breakfast remains one of my favorites. Whenever I'm fortunate enough to eat spiny lobster and avocado for breakfast I always think of Edwin and Marci Felton.

After breakfast, we drove to the A & B Fish house where I met fishermen and watched a fish house in full operation. I watched dozens of small boats unload their live harvest. I was amazed at the amount of spiny lobster unloaded from each boat. The lobstermen handled 100-pound boxes like they weighed ten pounds. Felton's uncooked (green) spiny lobsters were shipped to St. Petersburg or Miami at the end of each day during the main part of the season. On my first trip to Key West in 1964 spiny lobster fishermen were receiving 35 to 45 cents per pound for their delicious seafood product.

Felton was a "Conch's conch" easily recognized by his accent. The harmonic lilt of Edwin's enunciation of English was fascinating, unique and attention-grabbing. Edwin was born, raised and died in Key West. He and Marci had four wonderful children who helped them in the lobster and restaurant business up to the time the A & B Lobster House property was sold.

The Feltons participated in government and trade associations, trying to protect the commercial fishing culture. Edwin's father was a founding member of Southeastern Fisheries Association and served as president in 1955-56. Edwin followed in his father's footsteps serving as president in 1979-80.

During those short 25-years between his and his father's service, the face of Florida changed forever. Developers and land speculators destroyed a million acres of wetlands, forever. Fidel Castro seized Cuba in a bloody takeover. His military coup forced an exodus of two million hardworking Cuban exiles, seeking safe-haven in Florida from a communist dictator. Then Congress passed a law extending federal control of fisheries out to 200 miles, setting in place the opportunity for cultural genocide of the commercial fishing industry.

Even with all the misery going on in the fishing industry in Florida, life goes on. Edwin bought a used, forty-two foot yacht, with two big gasoline engines to make the trip to Fort Jefferson in less than four hours instead of ten on a shrimp boat or fifteen on the schooner. He and John Koenig, a banker who was a great friend of the fishing industry, ferried at least ten legislators back and forth to Fort Jefferson during the association's annual shrimping trip.

After Edwin received the title to his new toy, he had it notarized, then took the title and registration papers to the Monroe County Courthouse. He listed the new name of his boat as *Cojones,* which is Spanish for testicles. The Coast Guard official said he wasn't allowed to name a vessel *Cojones.* They told him to choose another name and reapply. Edwin was not a happy camper walking down the steps of the court house to his car. He went home and stewed over his dilemma for several hours.

The next morning he drove back to the courthouse with his amended registration papers. The new name of his boat would be the *C.O. Jones* and there was nothing the Coast Guard official or anyone else could do to stop him from naming it *C.O. Jones.*

He told me the next time I saw him that everyone at the court house burst out laughing except for the Coast Guard officials and the boys in Customs.

Every time I fished on the *C.O. Jones* I chuckled out loud with renewed respect for the intellect and wisdom of a Key West conch.

CHAPTER 8

Florida Marine Patrol in 1964

THE FLORIDA MARINE PATROL IN 1964 WAS DIFFERENT THAN IT IS TODAY. The association has worked well with the Marine Patrol ever since 1952 except for a four-year period in the mid 1970s during the rocky years when Eldon Gissendanner was the Director of the agency.

In 1964 Commander Gibson was Director of Law Enforcement for the Florida Board of Conservation. Gibson was one of the first men I met to offer our assistance in the quest for impartial law enforcement. Equitable law enforcement is a main objective of the Southeastern Fisheries Association.

Gibson was a straight-talking lawman with a raspy voice. His well chosen words sounded like they had to travel across sandpaper before reaching your ears. Many times I told him that he was tough as an old hickory log for a middle-aged, bald guy. He always smiled with a twinkle in his eyes and said, "You ain't too bad for a redneck bricklayer from St. Augustine yourself." There was mutual respect between us throughout his career. He served the people of Florida with honor and he is still missed by those who knew him.

Gibson's law enforcement division had eighty-eight law enforcement officers in 1964, including supervisory personnel. They had the formidable task of enforcing over two-hundred-thirty local saltwater fishing laws and statewide statutes. The Florida Board of Conservation officers were used anywhere in the state during any kind of emergency. I have chosen the Marine Patrol's St. Augustine assignment to illustrate the competence of the Marine Patrol in a tough situation.

Florida in 1964 was a political cauldron. The state had been reapportioned, breaking free from the Pork Chop Gang that controlled state government for decades. The Pork Chop Gang was a small group of North Florida senators who controlled all state money and appointments. In 1964 Congress enacted the Voting-Rights Act that created an ultra-conservative political constituency.

Dr. Martin Luther King led a protest against racial discrimination in St. Augustine in 1964. Commander Gibson's men were assigned the task of crowd control and protection of both black and white protestors by order of Governor Farris Bryant. Forty-three Board of Conservation officers, almost half of the entire force, were ordered to protect all citizens regardless of the color of their skin.

Gibson and his officers had to carry out their assignment during the hot, humid summer of 1964 as Dr. King and supporters marched the streets of St. Augustine protesting racial segregation. Dr. King's heroic effort in St. Augustine was a turning point against government-approved racial discrimination in the United States. Gibson and his officers helped turned the tide against racial hatred.

I don't know if the conservation officers sent to St. Augustine realized they were active participants in an important moment in U.S. history. The conservation officers were a piece of the drama protecting citizens fighting for equal rights. Dr. King and the US Supreme Court forced the nation to operate under the rule of law.

Racial tensions were high in St. Augustine where not-so-secret pockets of Ku Klux Klan members were still active. St. Augustine and Northeast Florida festered like boils on the butt of society. Racism is ugly. Hateful people are ugly. Gibson was the armed mediator between those who were taught to hate and those who demanded equal treatment. The Marine Patrol officers were professional.

The men under Gibson's leadership kept the Klan and segregationists from harming Dr. King or his supporters. That's something that couldn't be done four years later on the balcony of a hotel in Memphis, Tennessee where Dr. King was murdered in cold blood by a racist.

St. Augustine could have exploded into a full-blown riot except for the organized efforts of law enforcement officers and city leaders. Common sense, the presence of professional officers and strong political leadership by Governor Bryant prevailed over racial hatred. There were no lynch mobs in St. Augustine although some locals put a live alligator in the swimming pool where the civil rights leaders were staying. The motel and pool are gone, but there's a commemorative plaque located at the Hilton Bayfront Motel which is where the motel and pool were located.

Commander Gibson told a local reporter after the

St. Augustine assignment ended, "Law and order were maintained; there was not one casualty suffered by my officers and the rights of all persons were protected." I knew he was proud of the job his men performed during the toughest assignment of their careers. As hard as they worked in St. Augustine, the Marine Patrol received no time-off after they returned to their homes all over the state.

The Florida Cabinet quickly assigned most of the same officers during the three storms of 1964, Cleo, Dora and Isabel. The hurricanes made landfall, one after the other, flooding lowlands and isolating coastal communities and causing major damage inland. Downtown Live Oak suffered through twelve-foot high floodwaters.

Gibson's men handled the hurricane assignments in addition to marine resource enforcement responsibilities. They were commended by Senator Randolph Hodges, the Director of the Board of Conservation, as well as Governor Bryant for their competence and dedication. 1964 was a busy year for Gibson.

These special assignments turned out to be a key time for expansion of the Marine Patrol. Officers didn't usually carry weapons and lacked an efficient communication system. There were short-wave radio transmitters in each area's headquarters, but communication with officers in the field was sporadic.

In late 1964 new radios were installed in twenty-seven patrol boats. Everyone wanted radios installed in all watercraft before the end of the fiscal year.

The Florida Board of Conservation owned two

airplanes, a Cessna 182 assigned exclusively to law enforcement duties, and a Cessna 310 used for multiple duties including executive travel. It was normal for legislators to catch a ride on the Cessna 310 when it was headed in the direction they needed to go. There were no laws prohibiting legislators riding on state aircraft. This perk helped Hodges win appropriation requests for the Florida Board of Conservation in the legislative process because he had a chance to talk one on one with a decision-maker, a process he used often when he was the leader of the Pork Chop Gang.

The Florida Board of Conservation was also involved in international issues. The 1963 legislature passed a law prohibiting fishing in Florida territorial waters by boats registered in a communist nation. Shortly after the law took effect in 1964, the U.S. Coast Guard apprehended four Cuban fishing vessels in Florida territorial waters off the Florida Keys. The USCG escorted the Cuban vessel to Key West and turned the crew over to the Board of Conservation for prosecution under state law. There was a huge outcry from Cuban Dictator Fidel Castro and the U.S. State Department was promptly brought into the controversy. Men in dark suits came down from Washington and were seen in many of the popular watering holes.

After high-level wrangling and negotiations, the Cuban fishermen were tried under Florida law. They were convicted and the captains were fined $500. After the trial, the crew were returned to their vessels and escorted to international waters to return home. There were no further incidents of Cuban fishing boats violating the territorial waters of Florida.

A turning point in upgrading the Board of Conservation Law Enforcement Division came when it signed a contract with a federal agency to provide emergency services when needed. The mid 1960's was a pivotal time for the growth of the law enforcement capability and laid the groundwork for the creation of the Florida Fish and Wildlife Commission which has over 800 sworn officers protecting Florida wildlife and marine resources.

CHAPTER 9

The Fish Trap Era

I INTRODUCED TWO HIGHLY-EXPERIENCED TRAP FISHERMEN, DICK
NIELSEN AND BILL SANDIFER, AND THEIR SONS, BILLY AND RICHARD,
TO THE SOUTHEASTERN FISHERIES ASSOCIATION BOARD OF
DIRECTORS AT A MEETING IN KEY WEST. This simple introduction
and two hour discussion launched the association on a
twenty-year battle with divers and radical fishermen who
demanded everyone fish with rod and reel or spears and
bang-sticks.

Fish traps will always be highly controversial because
radical elements within the sport fishing industry despise
competition from a fish trap a net, or a hook and line
when used by a commercial fisherman. Some divers say
that it is unfair to catch a fish with a trap, but enjoy running a steel shaft through a grouper, snapper or anything
else swimming on the reefs. Is that fair? A dead fish is a
dead fish.

Militant outdoor writers called fish traps "Chambers
of Death". They never acknowledged that fish caught in
fish traps were random size and gender and could swim
in and out of the traps. Diving magazines were adamantly
opposed to the use of fish traps as were sport fishermen who illegally sold their catch through the back doors
of restaurants or retailers for cash under the cover of

darkness, a practice still prevalent throughout the state.

Radical angler organizations, led by a sport fishing magazine, directed an all-out political assault to ban fish traps through a misinformation campaign and staged photo ops.

Fake photographs showing a porpoise or undersized fish entangled in a net on a beach has been a media tool used to poison the minds of the masses for decades. The commercial fishing industry leaders and a deputy sheriff nearly caught the people who were using a dead whale as a photo op. They found the whale floating near shore in Southwest Florida. Anti-commercial activists laid a net over the bloated whale so incendiary photos could be published and commercial fishermen blamed. There was an allegation a marine patrol officer observed the entire incident.

If any state agency would have pursued this issue instead of letting politics rule what an eye-popping exposé it would have made in the world-wide press. It would have shown what some militants gladly do to support their ideology.

Fish trappers Dick Nielsen and Bill Sandefer were uncomfortable asking for help from fishermen from all over the state using other types of gear, but their livelihood was at stake. They spoke openly and honestly to an attentive Southeastern Fisheries Association's Board of Directors.

They explained why they used fish traps in the

deep, swift-moving water off Palm Beach and Broward Counties. They described, in great detail, how fish traps were constructed and how they worked. Some of the directors said trap use was just another way to harvest fish and didn't understand why others wanted to ban the traps.

Several members mentioned it did not matter how a fish is killed as long as the method is as humane as possible. Some members said they understood why angler groups wanted to ban fish traps and all commercial harvest because they wanted all the fish for themselves.

One board member observed there was only a handful of trappers and, with all the controversy surrounding this method of fishing, it might be politically wise for the association to endorse the prohibition of fish traps. The room got quiet for the few closing comments by Neilson and Sandifer. Then I was asked what I thought.

I said I hadn't read any scientific information leading me to support banning fish traps. The sport fishing writers called the fish traps all kinds of unsavory names but no legitimate marine biologist had concluded fish traps were harmful to the fish resource. I told the board there were only a few trappers asking for help and they were willing to accept stringent regulations such as daily reporting and oversight. I said banning a particular type of gear because other fisherman or sportswriters don't like it was not a valid reason for a ban in my opinion.

I asked one board member whom I respected very much what he would think if outdoor writers and a magazine publisher wanted to ban purse-seines that harvest baitfish just because there were only a few of them? He didn't answer my question, but looked me straight in the eyes and totally understood what I was saying to him.

After a few more minutes of discussion a motion was made by the man harvesting baitfish and duly seconded to support the fish trap fishermen to the fullest. The board voted unanimously in favor of the motion. A bitter name-calling-fight between the association and militants began at that moment. The fight continued for nearly two decades.

The Florida legislature, through the strong urging of House Speaker Ralph Haben and angler lobbyists, eventually banned fish traps in state waters, but could not ban them in federal waters as determined by a federal court.

The political fist fight in the Florida legislature was nasty because Representative Ralph Haben, a former friend of the commercial fishermen, was Speaker of the House and took a personal interest in passing a law banning fish traps. Haben's staunch opposition to fish traps was enhanced because a long time friend of his was lobbying for the Coastal Conservation Association. This made my job of killing the ban-the-fish-trap bill very formidable and in the end, impossible.

At one time in the battle we had the votes on the House Natural Resources Committee to kill the trap bill, but Haben added an extra member or two to the committee to swing the vote his way. He sat at the Natural Resources committee table when the vote was taken to watch the members of the committee vote. He glared at

Rep. Gene Hodges of Cedar Key who was the Chairman of the committee and a former commercial fisherman himself. Gene was the son of Randolph Hodges who was always in the fishermen's corner.

Even with Speaker Haben seated at the table, Rep Hodges argued forcefully and voted against the fish trap ban. The bill had another legislator's name on it, but it was the Haben bill and everyone knew it. I thought Hodges might sway enough of the members to join him, but his efforts fell short by one or two votes. Whether or not Haben punished Hodges for speaking against such an unjustified bill I don't know, but I lost respect for Haben for what he did to hard-working commercial fishermen of Florida. We had been friends before the fish trap controversy, but I never felt the same about him from that day forward.

The bill passed and was signed into law by Governor Bob Graham and with the stroke of the big pen, fish traps were banned from all state waters forever. There was no way to prove it, but rumor around the Capitol was that one lobbyist made $50,000 as his lobbying fee to ban fish traps. Fifty thousand dollars was a lot of money in those days for killing one fish bill. One lobbyist made $50,000 and scores of commercial fishing families were savaged. People who hurt other people for the fun of it aren't honest and should be avoided. A longtime state cabinet aide, turned high-powered lobbyist, said to me after the fight, "Bob, money talks and bullshit walks." I'm afraid he was right.

The fight to ban fish traps in federal waters began in 1977. John Green, a Gulf of Mexico Fishery Management Council member and successful oil-man from Beaumont, Texas, was the leader of the campaign to ban fish traps in the Gulf of Mexico. Green was a founding member of the Coastal Conservation Association and a former member of the Texas Parks and Wildlife Commission. Green served with Perry Bass, oil-baron from Fort Worth, who was a fanatic determined to ban commercial fishermen from catching red drum in Texas and later in the entire Gulf of Mexico.

Green and I were original members of the Gulf of Mexico Fishery Management Council. We were appointed by Secretary of Commerce Elliot Richardson in 1976 after Congress enacted the Magnuson Fisheries and Conservation Management Act, PL 94-265. We were good friends even though we were 180 degrees apart on the debate of "Who gets the fish?"

It took seventeen years before proponents of banning fish traps coerced the National Marine Fisheries Service to adopt plans to ban fish traps.

The National Marine Fisheries Service implemented a ten-year-phase-out of fish traps even though their own science proved fish traps had very little bycatch, did not harm the reefs and produced a high-quality fish.

During this time period the management councils were controlled by anti-fish trap and anti-commercial fishing members who didn't want the fish traps in the waters for another ten years. They demanded NMFS shorten the phase-out period. NMFS, to their credit, did not cave-in to the strong political pressure mostly from Texas. Try as it may, the Gulf Council leadership could not bully the other voting members to shorten the fish trap phase-out.

On March 18, 1999, the National Marine Fisheries Service notified the Gulf of Mexico Fishery Management Council that it had rejected the Council's proposal to accelerate the phase-out of fish traps off south Florida and prohibit their use after February 7, 2001 south of 25.05 degrees north latitude.

The official NMFS notice to the Gulf Council stated, "NO CONSERVATION BENEFITS HAVE BEEN DEMONSTRATED (for accelerating the phase-out), and THE MEASURE IS AN UNNECESSARY BURDEN ON FISHERMEN AND THE COSTS DO NOT APPEAR TO BE JUSTIFIED."

As a result, the use of fish traps was allowed to continue until February 7, 2007.

Those of us familiar with how a professional fish trap is utilized believe a fish trap is nothing more than an efficient piece of gear capable of producing high quality fish in a sustainable manner. The banning of fish traps, like the banning of gillnetting for mullet, is cultural genocide. There was no conservation benefit in banning inshore gillnets or fish traps. These unjust bans on fishing gear do nothing except ruin fishermen's lives and destroy seafood producing infrastructure in coastal communities.

CHAPTER 10

Long line fishing in Florida

LONGLINE FISHING WAS CONTROVERSIAL BEFORE FLORIDA FISH-ERMEN BEGAN USING THE GEAR IN THE 1970'S. Japanese tuna fleets used pelagic longlines in the Gulf of Mexico to catch giant blue fin tuna in the 1950's. Most citizens don't know there is a big difference between pelagic long lines, whose baited hooks are near the surface of the water, and bottom fishing long lines.

Longline fishing is efficient, relatively uncomplicated, but potentially dangerous to novice fishermen using it on small grouper boats. If fishermen don't use safe techniques they can become tangled up with the hooks. Fishermen have lost their lives after getting tangled in fishing gear peeling off the stern.

The Bureau of Commercial Fisheries, which was part of the Department of Interior in 1955, conducted longline surveys for commercial quantities of tuna and swordfish in the Gulf of Mexico and South Atlantic Ocean. Research cruises in 1955 aboard the *R/V Oregon,* documented by three deepwater-sets that one set caught a 300-pound blue fin tuna. The report said the blue fin tuna was in pre-spawning condition carrying immature eggs. They proved substantial schools of large blue fin tuna appeared in the Gulf of Mexico during February and early

March in preparation for spawning.

The United States was not the only nation aware of blue fin spawning aggregations. Japan's distant-water tuna fishermen were experts in longline fishing after WW II when challenged to feed their nation.

The Florida commercial fishing vessels, as well as charter boats fishing offshore, encountered Japanese vessels and watched them catch large quantities of fish using hundred mile longlines. Japanese fishermen utilized hand-blown glass buoys wrapped in large-mesh woven rope to keep the main line floating on top of the water.

Florida fishing boats cut the glass buoys from the line to sabotage the Japanese harvest. Much of the animosity might have been related to WW II which had ended less than a decade earlier. Fishermen brought the artistic glass buoys to shore as souvenirs and to brag about "stopping the Japs from taking our fish."

It's impossible to estimate the number of tuna, grouper and billfish the Japanese fleet harvested from the Gulf of Mexico during a period of no regulation and in an era where Japan was rebuilding its infrastructure to feed the nation. The Japanese freezer-vessels were at least 165 feet in length and capable of fishing at sea for a year or more.

The American longline boats were much smaller with far less holding capacity than the Japanese. The U. S. pelagic-longline fleet targeted swordfish, tuna and yellow-fin grouper. Later, the National Marine Fisheries Service strongly encouraged increased harvest of shark that was deemed under-utilized according to their scientific reports. The long standing philosophy of the National

Marine Fisheries Service of helping the commercial fishing industry changed dramatically when anti-commercial
fishing groups organized throughout the coastal areas of
the lower forty-eight states.

It did not take long for environmentalists to gain control of state and federal fisheries management. A once
healthy U.S. shark fishery was decimated. Draconian
regulations were enacted against American shark fishermen because foreign countries could not or would not
regulate their own shark fishing industry.

After a trumped up "Save the Swordfish campaign"
by one of the radical environmental groups was launched,
fishermen realized they were going to be demonized by
environmental groups paying for fake campaigns. The
environmentalist used a proven action plan; 1) capture
the media; 2) spread a big lie and repeat it in every way
possible; and 3) kill any science that does not support
their agenda. The Pew Trust and Environmental Defense
Fund are still using the action plan to the fullest and will
continue to do so until enough citizens realize they are
being bamboozled.

The swordfish in United States waters were never
endangered and the government knew it, but didn't have
the guts to speak out. After several years the U.S. swordfish industry and the National Marine Fisheries Service
created a program to reduce bycatch, initiate an on-going
education program within the fleet and continue participating in joint research efforts on swordfish.

As developing coordination with National Marine
Fisheries Service, the US swordfish industry was declared

a sustainable domestic fishery in spite of the environmentalists' opposition.

Win Rockefeller, John Mecom - owner of the New Orleans Saints - and Chris Weld of Massachusetts raised $500,000 to fund the Billfish Foundation at a meeting in Miami, Florida. The $500,000 war chest funded, by a few millionaires in a single evening, was more money than was ever spent on swordfish science in the South Atlantic. From a news story from the Miami Herald, May 1992, we read:

BILLFISH FANS CREATE CONSERVATION GROUP

"Discontent with fishing more but catching less was one of the concerns of a group of distinguished anglers and marine scientists who met this week at the Marriott Airport to organize the Billfish Foundation.

"This is not a political action group" said Winthrop Rockefeller, a big-time angler and one of the organizers. Among the 75 people who attended the organizational meeting was John Mecom of Houston, former owner of the New Orleans Saints, Chris Weld of Boston, Captain Dan Kipnis and Dr. William Fox of the Florida Marine Fisheries Commission. One area of concern is the impact of longline fishing and the introduction of nets. To help get the organization started, those attending gave $90,000 to open a bank account. "Besides the $90,000, we have $450,000 pledged among the Board members to the Foundation over the next few years", said Win Rockefeller. Jim Hardie, outdoor writer, The Miami Herald, May 1992, page 6E"

The real problem was never conservation or sustainability. The problem was a few wealthy sport fishermen wanted all the fish for themselves and were willing to pay whatever it took to provide their pleasure. Is this class warfare? You bet your rear-end it is.

Several decades have passed since the fake Save the Swordfish campaign and commercial fishermen are still harvesting swordfish with longlines in a few parts of the Atlantic Ocean. Sometimes the rule of law works.

CHAPTER 11

The Gulf and South Atlantic Fisheries Foundation

THE CREATION OF A COMMERCIAL FISHERIES DEVELOPMENT FOUN-
DATION, ENCOMPASSING VIRGINIA THROUGH TEXAS, WAS BORN IN
TALLAHASSEE, FLORIDA, IN 1976.

The Gulf and South Atlantic Fisheries Development
Foundation was established as an industry/government
program to conduct fisheries projects with a direct,
immediate impact for the improvement, growth and sustainability of the fish and fishermen.

The experience I had working for the U.S. Jaycees and
Southeastern Fisheries Association enabled me to draft a
non-political set of by-laws embraced by all commercial
fishing associations in the southeast. Bruce Morehead,
a dedicated National Marine Fisheries Service employee,
spent a week in Tallahassee offering sage advice for the
charter and by-laws which are still in effect in 2011. His
knowledge of transparency was instrumental in keeping
the foundation flourishing since 1976.

The timing for creating a fisheries development
foundation was perfect. Congress had just passed the
most far-reaching fisheries legislation in the history of
the nation. The law was enacted with lofty goals and

optimism for the domestic fishing industry. The purpose of the law was to provide a steady flow of seafood to the nation.

Congress voted to protect the US fishing industry from foreign fishing and simultaneously develop infrastructure for harvesting and processing fish by the domestic fishing industry.

Southeastern Fisheries Association provided initial organizational expertise and seed money to form the foundation. The original trustees were:

Bob Jones – Southeastern Fisheries Association
– President

Robert Mauermann – Texas Shrimp Association –
Vice President

Norman B. Angel – North Carolina Fisheries
Association – Secretary.

James W. Pace – Texas Seafood Distributors
Association – Treasurer.

James C. Farrelly – Louisiana Shrimp Association

Ralph Horn – Mississippi – at-large Delegate

Ralph Richards – Alabama Fisheries Association

Randall E. Dickinson – Alabama – at-large Delegate

Thomas R. Fulford – Organized Fishermen of Florida

George Y. Redding – Georgia's Fishermen's
Cooperative

Harold H. Von Harten – South Carolina's Shrimpers
Association

David Jones – Hilton Head SC Fishing Cooperative

George H. Harrison – National Blue Crab Industry
Association

THE GULF AND SOUTH ATLANTIC FISHERIES FOUNDATION

J. Keith Porter – Virginia Seafood Council
Thomas E. Reynolds – National Fish Meal & Oil
  Association

The first order of business was to select a head-quarters location and hire an executive director. Tampa was ideal because it was located in the center of the organizing states. It was close to the National Marine Fisheries Service headquarters in St. Petersburg and the foundation would be in the same building as the Gulf of Mexico Fishery Management Council. There was moder-ate debate over having the office in New Orleans and Charleston but the trustees overwhelmingly voted for Tampa as the headquarters.

I was selected to head the executive director's search committee. We received several outstanding résumés, but one stood out. Dr. Roger Anderson was working at the Virginia Institute of Marine Science and had a strong background in fisheries plus a good reputation for writ-ing grants. I contacted Dr. Anderson and arranged to meet him in Washington, D.C. in conjunction with a fish-eries meeting. There were two queen size beds in the hotel room where I was staying so I offered a bed to Dr. Anderson to reduce foundation costs. He accepted the offer.

He arrived late in the afternoon from Virginia. In our last phone call I told him what I looked like and he gave me his description, asking me to look for a hand-some young man with glasses and curly hair. We had no trouble recognizing each other when he walked into the hotel lobby where I was waiting. I recognized him by his glasses and curly hair. We shook hands then caught a taxi to a popular steak house in Georgetown.

We discussed every fishery in the southeast over a few scotch and water beverages. Dr. Anderson had a strong working knowledge about all of them. He knew the protocol for submitting and managing government grants. As an academician he knew the importance of accounting for every penny of a federal grant. I told him I was a stickler for transparency and the strict adherence of the foundation's bylaws, especially the Code of Ethics.

First and foremost the foundation cannot lobby, in Congress or state legislatures, using any foundation funds. Trustees working for trade associations could lobby on their own, but not on behalf of the foundation.

Second, no trustee is allowed to conduct business with the foundation. Compensation for trustees is limited to travel and per diem for official meetings. All reimbursements adhere to OMB and granting agency regulations.

Third, monies received, disbursed or held in all foundation accounts will be accounted for at all times and the books will be audited annually by a CPA. Roger had no trouble with these rules which the trustees had adopted at their organizational meeting.

I felt very good about the interview and believed the foundation would be hiring professional representation if Roger accepted the terms of employment offered by the Trustees.

When I was younger, and before there was mechanical assistance to help me breath better while sleeping, I was known as a world-class snorer, especially if I had a few ounces of good scotch before supper. I've been blessed since I was young with the ability to fall asleep within ten minutes of my head hitting the pillow. When Roger and I finished talking and solving all the fish problems in the world, I put on my pajamas, climbed in bed and turned off the light on my side of the room. Roger got into his bed a few minutes later.

I rolled over and said to him, "If you can, you ought to go to sleep right away because I'll be snoring shortly and I don't want to keep you awake." I turned back over and was asleep almost as soon as I closed my eyes.

The next morning I bounced out of bed and noticed Roger's bed was empty and without any covers. I headed to the bathroom, opened the door and there was Roger curled up in the bathtub with a pillow and blanket.

"What the hell you doing in the tub, son?" I asked him

"I never went to sleep," he lamented. "In my whole life I've never been in a room with so much noise. This porcelain tub, toilet paper in my ears and two bath towels stuffed in the crack under the door were my only refuge."

I don't think I laughed real hard at the time, but over the years describing our first meeting seems to get wilder with each telling. I felt bad when I saw that college professor curled up in the tub all because I made a little noise. I hoped he would still come to work for us.

He accepted the foundation's offer and began working

in Tampa within a month. Roger was tough. He fit in well with the foundation trustees.

During the first months of operation, the foundation received $250,000 from the Coastal Plains Regional Commission through the efforts of Dr. Claud Anderson, Regional Administrator of the US Economic Development Administration. The funds were distributed to state agencies and universities for programs of interest to the industry, especially a southern seafood marketing program for the Midwest part of the country.

Tom Murray followed Roger Anderson in 1984. Murray has worked diligently on behalf of the fishing industry for thirty five years. The economic models he developed in the early and mid 1990s told the real economic story of the Florida net ban saga.

During his tenure, the NOAA auditors descended on the foundation office and ran roughshod over Tom, Judy Jamison, his assistant at the time and members of the staff for almost three years. I felt the audit was politically motivated by a rogue bureau chief within the department. It was during the auditors "investigation" that I recognized those involved in such madness were like cretins wandering around a battlefield shooting the survivors.

One particular auditor who seemed to have a personal vendetta was Frank De George, Department of Commerce Inspector General staff, who, according to a note I got from Murray, ended up in a federal prison.

Murray remains jaundiced about the entire episode. He told me "the attack on my integrity basically was an attack on my breeding." Following his departure from the foundation in 1991, he filed a Freedom of Information request with U.S. Department of Commerce. After much delay and an additional appeal, the department admitted holding a total of seventy seven pages on the foundation "investigation," but would release only four pages that basically provided the name and address of the foundation. No question the "audit from Hell" was political and came from high up the U.S. Department of Commerce food chain. That is why they did not release the report. It took Tom and his wife Susan over a year to pay for the legal expenses related to the Freedom of Information request.

Judy Jamison was selected after Tom's tenure and currently serves as executive director. Judy and her professional staff of Gwen, Charlotte and Frank give continuity and dedicated service to the foundation trustees and the entire fishing industry. Judy is well respected for her honesty and integrity. Any person who has ever received a contract from the foundation on her watch knows all reports and records will be checked for full compliance of the law. The current era of the foundation will be described in the next edition of this Trilogy.

CHAPTER 12

The Thompson's of Titusville

CAPE CANAVERAL IS A UNIQUE PART OF FLORIDA. Its history is similar to St. Augustine's because Native American tribes lived on Florida's east coast for thousands of years before the arrival of Europeans.

Florida's earliest maps identify Cape Canaveral and the Keys as prominent navigational reference points. Spanish explorer Ponce de Leon, supposedly, came ashore in the Cape Canaveral vicinity in the early 1500's, but fierce tribes fighting hand to hand combat drove his men back to their ships and far away from their villages.

Fishing, hunting and gathering food from the sea was how the Ais Tribe lived as proven from bones, nets, hooks and artifacts found in middens along Florida's east coast. The fishing culture still exists but is under extreme stress.

I met Rodney Thompson in the 1970's. Rodney was worried that the rock shrimp resource he helped develop off Cape Canaveral would be overfished and maybe destroyed by the influx of huge trawlers from other states trawling twenty-four hours a day and seven days a week. Rodney worried that out-of-state vessels would tear up the fragile coral bottoms which locals avoided. His concerns were valid.

The Thompson families arrived in Titusville about eighty years ago. Rodney's parents migrated to Florida from South Carolina. Mary Jean's family were "saw-mill people" who cut railway ties for Henry Flagler's railroad while Rodney's grandfather was employed by the Florida East Coast Railroad. Mary Jean's family lived in a beautiful home which is now part of the Blue Springs State Park.

My grandfather, Robert Henry Jones, was a commercial gillnet and blue crab fisherman in Titusville according to the U.S. Census and anecdotal information. He probably knew the Thompson family.

Rodney's father owned a grocery store in the heart of downtown Titusville. He had a passion for fishing. When a new bridge was built in 1949, Rodney's dad, Herbert Sherrill Thompson, persuaded the city fathers to keep part of the old wooden bridge in place. He wanted it used as a fishing pier for locals and tourists who didn't own boats.

Herbert Thompson rented the pier from the city. He installed electric receptacles along the railings of the dock so people could plug in electric lamps, enticing big river shrimp to come to the lights.

When the shrimp swam on top of the water close to the light fishermen all along the pier cast their nets harvesting buckets of shrimp every night during the shrimp migration out of the rivers into the ocean. During the first 4th of July celebration weekend after the pier was opened, Rodney's daddy placed signs around town saying, "Fish at night with an electric light."

His promotion was a howling success. Families from Orlando, Cocoa, Daytona Beach and other cities drove to Titusville to catch a bucket of shrimp from the lighted fishing pier. It was a special evening for men, women and children to gather around the lights, watching the water and enjoying the cool summer breeze.

Thompson's innovative fish at night promotion added greatly to the economy of Titusville. Visitors bought goods and trinkets at local stores and ate in the seafood restaurants. The pier created a change of pace for Titusville night life where the radio and silent movie show had been the only entertainment available for years.

Every fishery in Florida was robust in those early years. The biggest problem was selling seafood, not harvesting it. The seafood industry boomed after World War II. The number of tourists increased each year giving much needed economic life to the entire state. New residents, many of whom were stationed in Florida during WW II or trained at Camp Blanding before joining the Normandy Invasion, began pouring into the state faster than highways, homes and schools could be built. Life was good.

Mary Jean and Rodney have been in love since they were teenagers. She accepted the fact Rodney was connected to the sea and always would be. She recently reminisced about an incident that happened when they were in high school. Rodney and a friend were on the beach watching a shrimp boat trawling near shore. On a lark they decided to swim to the shrimp boat and ask to get onboard. The crew members threw them a rope then helped them come up where they could stand on the stern deck to watch the shrimping operation during a short tow. As soon as the tow was over the crew members threw the boys overboard and told them to swim back home. It's a miracle Rodney made it back to shore because *"jaws"* usually follow shrimp boats. Mary Jean, all the kids and grand kids certainly are glad he made it back to shore.

Rodney and Mary Jean had four children, Laurilee, twins Tom and Tim and Sherri. Mary Jean was happy when Tim stopped longline fishing with Laurilee because she worried about them being at sea in all kinds of bad weather. They lost Tim when he was thirty-three years old in an accident at the Titusville boat building facility. His death was devastating to the family. They love Tim and hold his memory in the deepest recesses of their hearts. The hurt has slightly diminished, but will never go away. They are blessed that Tom and the girls are still very much in their daily lives.

Rodney was a Mercury outboard motor dealer in the 1950's. He was also building Critchfield Boats in Orlando. Building fiberglass sport fishing boats gave Rodney the expertise to design and build his world-famous T-Craft and later on the versatile and heavy-duty Thompson Trawler.

Thompson Trawlers and T-Craft boats are famous among professional fishermen throughout the country. They are extremely rugged boats capable of operating safely and efficiently in rough weather under harsh working conditions. The Thompson design and manufacturing specifications for T-Craft and Thompson Trawlers defy aging.

In the mid 1960's, Rodney was determined to build a 73-foot shrimp boat from a fiberglass-mold he knew about, owned by St. Joe Paper Company. The mold was stored in an open shed in Newport, Florida.

Rodney contacted Bob Brent, the St. Joe Company official in charge of projects in Northwest Florida. St. Joe owned the fiberglass mold and had a bad taste about building another fishing vessel after it lost money as partner in someone else's get-rich scheme. At first Brent was not interested in talking to another fisherman about a fiberglass boat building project using his mold.

However after Rodney pursued his proposal time and time again, Brent gave Rodney permission to use the mold. That's when the hard work began.

The mold was designed for the layers of fiberglass to be applied with the mold upside down. That meant applying fiber glass to the outside which was totally opposite of all other molds Rodney had ever worked on. Because he was such an innovator he knew he could build the sturdy shrimp boat using the "upside down" method.

He brought a crew of ten to fifteen men from his Titusville T-Craft plant to Newport. The days were hard, the nights were long, and there was a culture shock living in such a small, fiercely conservative community in the early 1960's. Not all of Rodney's employees were allowed to work or live in Newport and one was sent home to the safety of Titusville.

It took almost a year before the 73' fiberglass shrimp boat was launched. Rodney and his crew made the fiberglass thick, smooth and tough. The big white boat presented a unique gracefulness sliding down the rails then riding high in the calm river water.

L.C. "Ring" Ringhaver, builder of more shrimp boats than anyone in the world at his St. Augustine boat yard, watched the hustle and bustle that is part of launching a shrimp boat. Rodney said, "Ringhaver scurried around like a papa duck overseeing his ducklings." It wasn't his facility, but that didn't stop him from giving orders.

Near the last phase of construction, Rodney was strapped for cash and told Ringhaver he didn't have enough money to buy the engine, shaft and other parts necessary to finish the boat so he would have to wait a while to finish it.

Ringhaver listened, but didn't say anything. Rodney says in praise of Ringhaver, "In less than a week a new engine, shaft and all parts were delivered to the shed in Newport by Mr. Ringhaver." Ringhaver was a special breed of man who helped many fishermen during his lifetime.

Rodney built the boat on speculation and couldn't find anyone who wanted to buy a seventy-three foot fiberglass shrimp boat, ready to go to work.

Fishermen wanted either wood or steel. A bumper sticker popular at the time read, "If God wanted fiberglass boats, He would have made trees out of fiberglass."

Without a buyer, Rodney had no choice except return to shrimping as captain of the boat, himself. Off he steamed to Mississippi creating a much needed cash flow to pay his bills. He named the boat the *R.C. Brent*, in honor of the St. Joe official who had faith in him.

Rodney fished the boat in Mississippi long enough to pay off the debts then sold it to Ashland Oil Company which was considering expanding their portfolio into boat building.

Rodney built a 90-foot trawler for a client in Miami to make a cruise around the world. He only built one 90-footer, and then returned to building his thirty-foot T-Craft and forty-four foot Thompson Trawler.

Rodney built more than a hundred boats at his plant in Titusville before a fire destroyed the entire facility in 1983. The Thompson family decided not to rebuild. They concentrated on developing the Florida east coast rock shrimp industry and Dixie Crossroads Restaurant. In his spare time he tried to develop tuna fishing offshore Cape Canaveral.

When Rodney's was shrimping in the early 1960s he often caught twenty or more baskets of rock shrimp for every basket of brown shrimp. It didn't take a rocket scientist, even though a lot of them were moving to Titusville, to figure out the large abundance of rock shrimp available during certain times of the year.

Rodney was preparing to go shrimping one day when Captain Barrett of the Bureau of Commercial Fisheries Research Vessel, *Oregon II* walked over to him and said, "Rodney, follow me offshore and I'll make you a millionaire."

Rodney didn't say a word. He simply untied the lines of his boat and prepared to get underway. He followed the *Oregon II* to a certain spot, and then Captain Barrett called him on his radio phone and simply said, "Put your nets out, Captain Rodney."

After a short tow Rodney pulled the heavy nets up and dumped the massive catch on the stern deck. He called Captain Barrett and said, "I got a net full of peanuts," which is what the industry called rock shrimp in the early days.

Barrett responded, "Sell the peanuts and you'll be a millionaire."

As Rodney and his entire family found out, catching the peanuts would be much easier than selling them.

When Rodney and Mary Jean moved from their house by the old downtown Titusville pier to a new home, the kids weren't happy. They had grown up on, in and over the water at the pier. They loved their water oriented life very much and didn't want to leave it. Rodney tried his best to make the move as bearable as possible. He found an old pin-ball machine at a going out of business sale and brought it home for the kids. He fixed the coin box so all games were free. His kids and their friends in the neighborhood became world-class pin ball machine players.

Laurilee, the oldest Thompson child, said her daddy would be offshore shrimping for five days at a time, and although they loved him very much, they hated to hear his old banged-up pickup truck pull into their driveway. They knew he would put a big bucket of rock shrimp on the kitchen table and then challenge everyone to figure out how to get the meat out of the rock-hard shells.

Working with shrimp that smelled like mud was not a favorite pastime for the kids who wanted to be playing ball or riding horses or tending to the myriad wild critters in their back yard. Instead, when daddy put the shrimp bucket on the table, everyone worked figuring out an easy way to get the meat out of the shell.

During one of the brain storming sessions at the kitchen table Laurilee said, "Why don't we split 'em and broil 'em? Everyone says they taste like lobsters anyway." She reached in the silverware drawer, pulled out a serrated knife and sawed the rock shrimp in half. She pulled the sand vein out exposing nothing but white meat. The rest is history.

The Thompson family figured out the way to get to the meat. Now they had to figure out a way to sell 'em. The sales team was composed of the same folks who were the processing team. Consequently, the kids, mom and dad performed hours and hours of hard work in the kitchen splitting rock shrimp.

Miss Ella owned a well known local bar and grill and

became the Thompson's first paying customer. The hand-processed rock shrimp were salty, so the bar patrons ate salty shrimp and drank more beer. Miss Ella was happy and her bar patrons were happy. So was the Thompson family.

They didn't realize it, but this was the same marketing program the New York bars used when they started selling shrimp from Fernandina and St. Augustine at the beginning of the twentieth century. Tasty, salty shrimp increase beer sales.

Not long afterwards, Bill Mayfield's Neptune Inn in Rockledge became a very big customer. The Florida rock shrimp era began with gusto in the early 1970's. People drove many miles to eat the rock shrimp at the Neptune Inn.

Ed Joyce of the Florida Department of Natural Resources presented a paper at the Twenty-Seventh Annual Session of the Gulf and Caribbean Fisheries Institute in November 1974 on Rock Shrimp Research and Marketing. Florida was promoting the utilization of rock shrimp as part of the overall state economic development programs and the work Ed Joyce performed was critical to the long term sustainability of the rock shrimp fishery.

The Vona family was among the first fishermen harvesting rock shrimp in a big way. Sam Vona was a fishing pioneer who remained in the Florida shrimping industry all his life. Between Captain Vona, Captain Buffkin and Captain Sterling Rodney had six boats catching rock shrimp for his growing company.

The increased production and value of rock shrimp occurred before the United States shrimp market was overwhelmed with pond-raised shrimp from all over the world. The biggest hurdle to higher success was splitting the rock hard shrimp shell quickly without losing any meat.

Too many boats trawled in areas that should not have been trawled so it didn't take long for the rock shrimp fishery to approach overfishing status. Florida rock shrimpers went through a tough political period because of damage done to some sensitive reef areas that should have been closed to trawling from the beginning. That is another story for another time, but this chapter has one more incident.

Laurilee Thompson is co-owner of Dixie Crossroads in Titusville, one of Florida's most famous restaurants for good seafood. When she was a teenager she had an idea of putting multiple baited-hooks on a sturdy line and dropping it in the ocean so she could catch more fish per trip. Laurilee was a fisherman since she could walk. She and her friend Angie Ciell tried "tub trawling," an experiment they dreamed up using a plastic tub to hold coiled up line and hooks – and using it in 100-fathoms of water.

Laurilee recalls her first longline experience. As soon as their equipment was ready, they starting dropping their "longline" overboard. The swift current quickly pulled the line, bait, hooks and tub from their hands and everything disappeared immediately. Their first longline experiment failed.

A CULTURE WORTH SAVING

It was a much different story for Laurilee in 1981 when she proudly captained the *Mary Jean*, a sixty-five-foot Thompson Trawler named for her mother. It was a powerful, efficient boat built by her dad and powered with a 671 Detroit Diesel engine. The *Mary Jean* held 30,000 pounds of ice and in those days they carried a pound of ice for each pound of fish they hoped to harvest.

The *Mary Jean* fished about 140-miles off Fort Myers and was one of the first longline boats fishing for yellow-edge grouper. During the first two years she harvested nearly 40,000 pounds of fish in seven days using a twelve mile longline.

"There was a fish on almost every hook," she told me. "We never saw one turtle while fishing there." She added, "Some months most of the fish were full of roe."

She unloaded her catch at Erickson and Jensen's shrimp docks in Fort Myers Beach. The fish were re-iced and trucked to Heber Bell & Sons in St. Petersburg, who bought them for one dollar per pound.

In less than two years, her weekly harvest dropped from 40,000 pounds to 7,000 pounds even though she increased the length of her longline to 40 miles. Instead of a five-man crew she changed to a three-man crew because of less production.

She believes she and other longline fishermen found a virgin population of yellow-edge grouper. The early harvests were phenomenal as would be the case in a virgin fishery. She continued to fish in other areas until she got her fill of the offshore fishing life and the constant hassle by federal law enforcement agents, especially one customs agent who told her he would plant pot on the boat if that was what it took to get her out of the area.

Laurilee told me about an incident that happened around 1982, well before the state and federal governments regulated most commercial fishing boats in the southeast out of business.

Florida longline fishing boats routinely tied up at the Truman Docks in Key West. The dock was convenient and the fee reasonable. Captain and crew could catch a taxi to town for rest and relaxation after several weeks at sea or they could go buy a bag of cheeseburgers and bring them back to the boat, if that was their desire.

The only draw back to tying up at the Truman docks was the dock master required a portion of the "shack fish" i.e. fish the crew were given by the boat owner which was traditional in most Florida fisheries. The dock master wasn't the friendly sort according to Laurilee. He rode around the property like the 'cock of the walk' in his golf cart, giving fishermen orders.

Most boat crews dutifully handed over a portion of their fish to the dock master, but the crew on one boat, captained by a hardnosed northerner with a long black pony tail, refused to pay tribute. They were big men, rough, unshaven and hard workers, but a couple had a penchant for doing things different than the law allowed. The name of the boat might have been *Titan* or *Olympic"* or something like that, but the name doesn't matter.

Captain Laurilee Thompson was tied up to the ship in question because it was the only spot available. She and her crew, including her younger brother Tim, were cleaning up and preparing for the next trip when all of a sudden they heard loud, threatening voices and several men arguing.

She stood up on the gunnels and saw the dock master surrounded by the burly crewmen from the boat she was tied up to. She watched in stunned silence as they picked up the electric golf cart with the dock master still sitting on the front seat. They tossed everything over the seawall and into the sea. The splash of a golf cart – amid the curses and wailing from the passenger still sitting in it -created a unique sound like she had never heard before or since.

The fishermen were laughing their heads off as the dock master and cart sunk slowly to the bottom. He was still yelling as his hat slowly floated away from his head.

Captain Laurilee's crew quickly untied their lines and eased away from the other longline boat and headed out to sea. The other boat did the same just ahead of the blue lights and just as the dock master and golf cart were retrieved.

Laurilee doesn't recall the longline boat with the pony-tailed captain and burly crew going back to the Truman Docks, but she returned to Key West six months later and tied up at the Truman Docks. Her brother Tim desperately wanted a big bag of McDonald's cheeseburgers. After the boat was secured Tim walked to a nearby public phone booth to call a taxi. While he was in the phone booth a friendly groundskeeper came to Laurilee and told her longline boats couldn't tie up there anymore. And, the City Police were on their way to arrest her because of her association with the crewmen who performed the illegal baptism of the dock master.

Tim was in the phone booth and Laurilee started yelling for him to get onboard because the police were coming to arrest them. Tim really wanted a cheeseburger so he hesitated for a moment to analyze the situation. The other crew member was begging Laurilee to leave, but she didn't want to leave her brother.

They finally untied the lines. Tim thought he would be left behind so he took off running for the boat as fast as he could. Laurilee was ten yards from the dock when Tim dove as far out into the water as he could. She tossed him a rope then darted back into the wheelhouse and pushed the throttle forward. Tim hung on with all his might.

What a scene that must have been with the *Mary Jean* getting away from the police while pulling a young man through the water without a ski, inner tube, or even a life vest.

Tim was finally pulled aboard about 100 yards from the dock. After catching his breath and pushing the hair out of his eyes he joined in the laughter. The belly-busting moment had them all rolling on the deck laughing in such a way that only happens a few times in a lifetime.

Laurilee Thompson retired from fishing in 1987, ending a love affair with the sea that started as a young girl playing and fishing on a dock in Titusville.

CHAPTER 13

Oak Hill

COMMERCIAL FISHING IN OAK HILL BEGAN AROUND 1908. The quaint fishing village is located on the banks of the Indian River Lagoon in southeast Volusia County, east of U S 1. Oak Hill is known for big trout, bull redfish and mullet that were caught with gillnets for over 100 years by local fishing families before nets were banned in 1995. The home-made, painted plywood tunnel boats used for decades were small and easy to operate. They had such a shallow draft that they could almost fish in wet mud. The fat mullet have a distinctive sweet taste. Those who eat Oak Hill fried mullet believe the special taste comes from the pure water in the undeveloped estuaries of the Indian River Lagoon.

I met Millard Goodrich and Bud Dewees during the mid-1960s. They were gillnet fishermen first and businessmen second. I had the pleasure of their company, wisdom, humor and practical political knowledge until they died. Bud Dewees was a raw-bone, thin, bushy-headed fisherman who smiled instead of frowning. He owned LeFils Fish Camp that served sport fishermen from all over the state. They rented his boats and motors and bought live shrimp to catch gator trout and trophy redfish. Bud Dewees was quick-witted and a born mediator.

A CULTURE WORTH SAVING

One evening my friend Harmon Shields and I were at Bud's camp on our way back to Tallahassee after a meeting in Miami. Bud was preparing to go gillnet mullet fishing at one of his favorite honey-holes. Harmon was going with him that evening while I was going to St. Augustine to visit family and friends. Before I left Oak Hill I pigged-out on fresh, fried, fat, east coast-mullet and cheese grits that melted in my mouth. Bud enjoyed catching fat roe-mullet with his gillnet this time of the year. I'm always curious about why people do certain things and I knew Bud Dewees enjoyed what he did by his passionate words.

"Bud, what's the best thing you like about mullet fishing?" I asked figuring he was going to respond in deathless prose about being out in his tunnel-boat darting across the smooth water in the dark of night, watching the countless stars in the heavens and enjoying the cool, fragrant river-breeze slightly stinging his whiskered face.

"Well Bob, I like being on the water in my tunnel-boat and I'm glad Harmon is going with me tonight, but the best thing is knowing every time I grab the net and shuck a mullet into the fish box, it's like somebody sticking fifty-cents in my pocket," he said. "Where else can a man do what he loves and put a fifty-cent piece in his pocket for every fish he harvests?"

There was nothing I could say, but I filed his words away and have thought about his answer many times during my life. What he said is harvesting fish creates wealth the same as farming or mining. When a mullet is harvested and sold, it immediately creates wealth and as that fish makes its way through the marketing chain from the water to the waiter, it becomes more valuable. Commercial fishing creates wealth; recreational fishing expends wealth earned elsewhere. Nicely stated Bud Dewees.

The Goodrich family is a Florida heritage family and one of the first to settle in Oak Hill in the late 1890's. Millard Goodrich was my main political contact for the family. He was the spokesman on fisheries issues. He often testified to the Florida legislature or any governmental body having authority over fisheries. He spoke with humility, always polite and sincere. He usually bowed his head when he was addressing the legislators in his low voice. He had a ruddy complexion that comes from years on the water. He was balding with blondish hair and always wore a suit and tie out of respect for the legislative process and those who controlled his livelihood.

He was not a polished orator as he stood erect before a legislative committee, but his words defined wisdom and his unashamed love for the culture of his ancestors as well as young mullet fishermen hoping to live their lives in the fishing industry. Little did the Oak Hill fishermen know their world would be ripped apart when radical anglers groups, a cadre of outdoor writers and a sport-fishing magazine poisoned the minds of Floridians by painting commercial fishing as the lowest form of human endeavor.

Millard's father and uncle founded the Goodrich Brothers Fish Company in the 1920's. The history of Oak Hill is similar to many other Florida communities that started out cutting timber, growing oranges, making turpentine and fishing commercially. The "hunters and gatherers" were well-respected members of any community because they provided food and jobs. Because they were held in high-esteem for so many years, the Florida legislature supported them and listened to them when land speculators wanted to shut them down to build marinas, condos and gated communities. These developers did not want to see a commercial fisherman anywhere near them or their guests.

When I began lobbying for the seafood industry in 1964, Representative James H. Sweeney represented Volusia County. He was the Dean of the House and an absolute gentleman. He was supportive of the commercial fishermen in Oak Hill and protected them from being put out of business by developers and sport fishing radicals. Sweeney was a wise and kind legislator representative who is still missed.

I think it was in the 1970s when Senator Bill Gillespie, D–Volusia County, introduced a local bill that would decimate gillnet fishermen in Oak Hill. Millard Goodrich, Bud Dewees and others drove to Tallahassee, joining me for a meeting in Senator Gillespie's Tallahassee office. We pleaded with him to withdraw his local bill and work with the fishermen on a compromise to solve his perceived problem that the commercial fishermen were catching all the fish. The senator was unwilling to consider a compromise and told us no. He said he was going to pass the bill whether we liked it or not. In those days that was not a nice thing to say to your constituents.

As we stood to leave, I told him we would oppose his bill and reminded him the Volusia County House of Representatives delegation was not supporting his bill.

Senator Gillespie said he did not care what others did. He got angry when I told him we would be speaking against his local bill and would work against it.

We told him his bad bill would keep his local fishermen from making a living they had pursued since Oak Hill was founded. We told him mullet fishing in Oak Hill was a valuable culture, sustainable and highly regulated because of the mesh size requirements in gillnets, closed fishing seasons and minimum fish size. We reiterated, in a civil manner, the fishermen harvested mullet after they had spawned at least once and probably twice thereby perpetuating the continuation of the resource. We showed him, through state and federal landing statistics, that the annual mullet harvest in Oak Hill did not harm the fishery.

Our arguments and pleas fell on deaf ears. Senator Gillespie drew a line in the sand with his legislative sword. We knew the relationship between Gillespie and the fishing industry would turn hostile, but there are times you fight for what you believe in no matter the consequences.

Gillespie quickly passed his local anti-commercial fishing bill in the Senate without opposition, which was senatorial courtesy for senator's local bills. But when it was sent to the House in Messages from the Senate, the Speaker assigned it to the Natural Resources Committee. Gillespie was incensed. He wanted his bill placed on the

Local Bill Calendar and approved without discussion because that was how local bills were normally treated.

In due course, but not immediately because I was trying to bottle the bill up until the session ended, Chairman A.H. "Gus" Craig, (D) St. Augustine, scheduled Gillespie's bill for a committee hearing. When the meeting was called to order, Chairman Craig recognized Senator Gillespie to explain his bill. He made a few cursory remarks about the need to stop commercial fishing to protect the resources, but basically told the committee to pass his local bill that only affected his county.

It was uncommon for a lobbyist to speak against a legislator's local bill because it made the legislator mad as hell, but the Senator's bill was anathema, unfair, not needed and our side needed to be on the record.

I reluctantly submitted a card to speak against the bill so Representative Craig called on me after Senator Gillespie's testimony. I explained our objections from the fishermen's point of view. I pointed out Oak Hill fishermen were primary producers of mullet and their harvest furnished mullet to a large number of minority retail fish markets as well as small retail markets up and down the east coast. I testified the bill was not a conservation measure, but a bill to ban commercial fishermen from harvesting fish at the request of anglers. I asked the committee to vote against passage of a bad bill.

During my testimony, Senator Gillespie's face turned crimson and his eyes were ablaze. When I concluded, but before the vote was taken, he jumped from his seat, mad as a wet hen, looked at me and said,

"You only represent five crooks in Oak Hill and I represent 250,000 citizens of Volusia County."

I looked him straight in his eyes and said,

"I have seven members in Oak Hill and they are going to be upset when I phone them in a minute and tell them you called them crooks."

The Committee voted overwhelmingly against Senator Gillespie's bad bill and he stormed from the room. True to my pledge I called Bud Dewees and Millard Goodrich and told them Senator Gillespie called them crooks at the Natural Resources Committee. They said they would make sure the Senator would hear from the Oak Hill community and all others they could contact in Volusia County who bought fresh seafood each week.

Suffice to say Senator Gillespie was not happy with me and was not happy when he faced the citizens in Oak Hill. The Senator was caught up in the heat of battle and could not accept the fact his local bill was defeated, setting a precedent for testifying against bad local bills after that session.

Bud Dewees and Millard Goodrich were an important part of my life. There was always a problem to solve in Oak Hill, but they were blessed with local legislators who understood the culture such as T.K. Wetherell who went on to become President of Florida State University and Sam Bell who remains in the legislative process as a prominent and successful lobbyist. Both Wetherell and Bell were generally sympathetic to the plight of the commercial fishermen when they were legislators. We were grateful for their help.

A CULTURE WORTH SAVING

Since the formation of the Marine Fisheries Commission and the net ban was placed in the state constitution in 1995 and the creation of the Florida Fish and Wildlife Commission, the proud fishing industry that sustained Oak Hill for so many decades is nothing but a memory. It is still a fabulous fishing area and a developer with a heart saved a portion of the fishing culture by not building wall to wall condo's and a gated community where the land and water is reserved for the wealthy. The demise of the Oak Hill fishing community is a blemish on any society that emphasizes waterfront homes for the few over protecting and harvesting renewable natural resources for the many.

CHAPTER 14

My First fishing experience – Mullet Every Way

WHEN THE SUN DROPPED OUT OF SIGHT BEHIND WEST AUGUSTINE AFTER THE EVENING MEAL AND THE CRY WENT OUT THAT THERE WAS MULLET ON THE BEACH, FAMILIES JUMPED IN THEIR CARS AND HEADED TO ST. Augustine Beach. Everyone drove with their windows down, relishing the cool air flowing through their hair. It was 1941.

TV's weren't invented. If they had been, only the business owners or retired Florida East Coast railroad officials could have afforded to buy one. For the kids lucky enough to earn fifty cents from cutting a yard or cleaning up around a service station, the treat of the week was going to the Jefferson Theater on Saturday morning. They knew Gene Autry, Champion and Smiley Burnette always beat the bad guys in the black hats and Roy Rogers and Dale Evans would sing a song or two. Locals with homemade dune-buggies would ride through soft sand on high sand dunes headed for the old, rickety drawbridge leading to Vilano Beach. Catching mullet with a cast net was a happy and festive event and gave working folks a chance to eat fresh fish during and following the Hoover Days as well as during World War II food shortages. When mullet were bountiful, a car's spotlight could locate massive schools of fish swimming leisurely in the waves. The mullet was stacked like cord wood. What a sight it was for me and my brother Richard.

My daddy had a shiny, jet black 1935 Ford coupe with a red leather rumble seat. The rumble seat was big enough for me, Richard and the scratchy, fish-smelling Purina Feed croaker sack that would soon be filled with fresh mullet.

If you've never ridden on a red leather rumble seat, wind blowing on your face, and gasping for breath if you stick your head outside the protection of the car, you haven't lived. The drive across St. Augustine's Bridge of Lions in a rumble seat is exhilarating. We felt as high as the clouds and saw the outline of the city and miles of the Matanzas River in both directions. The road to the beach had two narrow lanes. When there was the cry of "mullet on the beach" a steady stream of powerful V-8 autos and trucks headed for the narrow wooden ramps at St. Augustine Beach.

When daddy reached the hard-packed sand off the ramp near the fishing pier and old hotels, he turned north towards the inlet. He idled along at the edge of the water, head lights off, while we listened to the soft roar of the surf and the sweet sounds of twin exhaust pipes. Daddy flicked his spotlight on every once in awhile, searching for mullet in the waves or leaping in the air.

When daddy saw a fat, torpedo-like mullet jump, he turned the car in the direction it was jumping and drove fifty yards ahead of where he saw the jump and stopped. Daddy was only five-foot-five, but he grabbed his eight-foot English cast net and sprinted barefoot on the sand to the spot he thought the mullet were swimming.

Daddy waded up to his chest and threw directly into the wave when the foam was on top of the water. The mullet couldn't see the net coming. He instantly felt big, roe-laden mullet slamming into the net before the lead sinkers hit soft sand. He quickly pulled the hand line to tuck the net and capture the fish in the bag. Daddy grinned as he struggled just a little bit with a net full of roe mullet, the same way his Seminole ancestors did centuries ago.

It would be over two decades before I experienced that special feeling of casting my net over a big school of mullet while my children followed pulling a croaker sack along St. Augustine Beach.

Daddy ran back to where we were cheering, jumping up and down holding the scratchy, brown croaker-sack. When he shucked the fish from his net, they flipped and flopped and tried to get back in the water. "Get the damn fish in the sack," Daddy said with that deep serious tone in his voice when he meant business. "Yes sir," we replied simultaneously.

Richard and I bumped into each other and stumbled trying to keep the mullet close to the bag and away from the water. We grabbed them with our little hands, trying hard to put them in the sack. We quickly found out mullet don't have teeth, but their fins can punch a hole in small fingers and it hurts like the devil.

We had just put the last slippery mullet in the sack when daddy brought another net full. He saw blood on our fingers. "Rub sand on the cuts and fin holes, then pull the bag down the beach," he said as he ran back into the water to catch more fish. Sometimes daddy would stutter, but never when he was catching mullet or working on a car engine or transmission. We did what daddy told us and did it in a hurry. If we didn't, our butts would be red and sore.

After nine or ten more successful casts, the croaker sack was full and impossible for us to drag along the sand, no matter how hard we tried.

Daddy smiled at us trying to pull the heavy bag that wouldn't budge. He easily picked up the catch and set the one-hundred pound sack of mullet on the rubber mat in the rumble seat. We headed home.

We had fish scales in our hair, our clothes, stuck behind our ears, our bare legs and canvas sneakers. We smelled salty and fishy. It was awesome, and I still yearn for the chance to catch mullet on St. Augustine Beach. Richard and I felt like the best fishermen in the world. We almost froze to death in the rumble seat crossing the Bridge of Lions with the cool September air blowing across and up our wet shorts and T-shirt.

Daddy had the radio on WFOY-AM and was smoking a Lucky Strike cigarette. We knew he was happy by his smile and the way he helped us into the rumble seat. His powerful left arm and elbow rested on the door as the wind blew through the front part of the car. He steered with his left finger and held the cigarette in his other fingers or let it hang from his lips. Daddy was a rough man with a big heart.

MY FIRST FISHING EXPERIENCE – MULLET EVERY WAY

When we returned to our house at 146 Cunningham Drive, family and neighbors gathered to help clean the fish and share in the bounty. I remember Mama making us take off all our clothes before coming in the house. We did what Mama said without hesitation and streaked to the bathtub laughing and giggling in our birthday suits. We had fish roe and grits for breakfast and fried fish and more grits for supper. We ate mullet every way possible until it was all eaten up. Then we were all ready to go again.

Mullet fishing with a cast net is a southern art form. It's as exciting as fishing for grouper or bass or sailfish. The excitement starts building long before you make the first cast of the net. The lucky ones, like me, are fishing in our minds three or four days before we put the net in the truck. We dream about the big-cast when you net fifteen or twenty two pound roe mullet and take them home so you can have friends over to celebrate your success as a hunter and gatherer, as well as enjoy the delicious bounty of your harvest. When I walk along the shore, mullet fishing early in the morning or late in the day with a cast net, fish-sack and a loved one, I am transported back in time, thoughts and pleasant emotions.

Mullet fishing will always be a popular, important cultural event in Florida coastal areas. There is a unique taste of fresh, fried mullet which is enhanced by the aroma of marsh grass and the chill of the air.

I will always love the gritty taste of the salt and sand on the sinker that I put between my teeth as I cast the net in a perfect circle. I marvel at my wrinkled hands and feet after wading in saltwater for several hours. I delight in being wet up to my chest, walking along the shore and thanking God I'm still able to fish.

CHAPTER 15

Florida outdoor writers

THE RELATIONSHIP BETWEEN COMMERCIAL FISHERMEN AND RECRE-
ATIONAL FISHERMEN IN FLORIDA HAS BEEN STRAINED AND VOLATILE
SINCE THE 1800'S WHEN FLORIDA'S FIRST OUTDOOR WRITERS
TOUTED THE STATE AS THE MECCA FOR SPORT FISHING HALF THE
TIME AND RAILED AGAINST COMMERCIAL FISHING THE OTHER HALF.
Some considered themselves journalists though in real-
ity they were biased writers promoting sport fishing and
condemning commercial fishing. The openly biased ones
should have been writing for a non-government organiza-
tion instead of newspapers.

Their propaganda poisoned the minds of hundreds of
thousands of newspaper readers around the state against
commercial fishing. Their unrelenting desire to have all
the fish allocated to their friends led to the oxymoron,
"Everyone likes to eat seafood, but don't want commercial fishermen to harvest it."

Heber Bell, SFA President, called me in March of
1965 and said I should attend a meeting in Tampa to
discuss a proposal making king mackerel a game-fish.
He said the anti-commercial groups wanted to designate king mackerel as a game fish and prohibit sale. I
told him that was a dumb idea and asked why anyone
wanted to do that. He told me to attend the meeting

and listen to Bob Ingle who was Director of Research for the Florida Board of Conservation.

I left for Tampa early the next morning, listening to good music and singing songs with Roger Miller or Gary Lewis and the Playboys. Anyone who saw me speeding through Perry, Old Town or Cross City in my faded blue 4-door Chevy Impala would have thought I was happy. They would have been correct. I was free of any wide and deep scars from fish battles in the legislature and was as naive as anyone would be without any experience dealing with high-level politics. I thought if something was unfair it wouldn't be done. It took almost five decades to convince me that some folks do unfair things all the time just to demonstrate their political power. I was glad Bob Ingle would be at the meeting to guide me.

I first met Bob Ingle around 1950 or 1951 when he visited Representative Charlie Usina at his family's cabin on the St. Johns River. I was in high school and dating Mr. Usina's daughter whom I married in 1955. Ingle was a large, muscular, gregarious marine scientist. He was a father-bear at the lab and watched over it with eyes so clear and tongue so sharp he could shred a novice biologist with one sentence. He spoke the English language using words and phrases totally strange to my background and limited education.

There was a ritual at the Usina river cabin that at 5:00 o'clock sharp, the beer mugs and scotch glasses were brought forth from the cabinet and the cocktail hour or two was convened. After the adults fixed their drinks we all walked out to the tin-roofed area at the end of the dock. I loved sitting on a cypress bench in front of the Usina's barn-red board and batten cabin, listening to Bob Ingle's fascinating stories about strange people and stranger critters or vice versa.

At some point in the conversation Papa Usina told Ingle, "Yea I know... all you need is a little more time and a lot more money." Ingle always responded with a smile. And Representative Usina always helped the lab get a good appropriation.

Once, at Ingle's house off Mission Road in Tallahassee, we were having a delightful conversation. After a few months experience I was able to discuss most fisheries' issues with a modicum of intelligence based on what I was learning everyday. We were discussing the drastic impacts on fish stocks from water pollution that was killing sea grasses, oysters and clams and how Florida citizens were being physically harmed by air and water pollution. While sipping a scotch and water he set his glass on the bar, looked at me with a serious face and said, "Bob, our bodies are being infused and inundated with carcinogenic compounds."

I looked at him, exhaled the strong deep-puff from my Marlboro cigarette and said, "What?"

I was coming up the learning curve, but not fast enough to understand carcinogenic compounds. He merely picked up his highball and told me more about the birds and the bees of the fisheries world. That's what I call a mixed metaphor.

Over the years I have used his sentence in several perfect situations and often whomever I am talking to gives me a quizzical look. Each time using his words I feel the essence of Bob Ingle and it makes me feel like an intellectual.

The meeting to discuss making king mackerel a game fish was held at the Hillsborough County Court House in downtown Tampa. When I found the room and walked in, I saw Bob Ingle. I put my battered Samsonite briefcase on the conference table next to where he was sitting. We shook hands and he thanked me for attending. He evidently talked to Heber Bell and that was probably why I was told to be there and oppose the game fish status for king mackerel.

I didn't think I could add much to the meeting because I was so new to the fish world, but the reputation of Southeastern Fisheries Association was such that its involvement in any fishing controversy made a difference. I did not realize the importance of a fisheries organization in the world of Tallahassee politics and I did not realize what a good reputation the association enjoyed thanks to its fourteen years of honest work. I did not know it, but there was political muscle, corporate knowledge and regional clout among the members of the association.

The group sitting around the polished mahogany table included a fishing writer for the *Tampa Tribune,* Bob Ingle, Chief of the Florida Board of Conservation marine lab, a few folks representing the Florida League of Anglers and a hook and line king mackerel fisherman who wanted to become a charter boat operator. There were other people present, but I can't recall their names or associations, but they all played significant roles in forming my professional life and setting the stage for the intense fish wars which were about to explode in Florida and all other states bordering the Gulf of Mexico and South Atlantic Ocean.

When they started talking about "the estuary" I thought they were talking about a place for birds. I didn't say much because I didn't know much. I felt like the person Winston Churchill wrote about when he said, "A modest little person, with much to be modest about." I kept copious notes trying to figure out their immediate and long term goals. Bob Ingle carried "my water" and did it from a scientifically based perspective. After a half-hour into the meeting, you did not need to be a rocket scientist, or even a biologist, to figure out the anglers wanted all the fish. The outdoors writer used his bully-pulpit at the *Tampa Tribune* newspaper to condemn commercial fishermen. He misused his position as a newspaper writer to advance the cause of his angler friends. He used it well for many years and tainted the reputation of the commercial fishing industry in almost every column he wrote. His wish was to confiscate the public marine resources from non-boaters and reserve them exclusively for anglers. It was really that simple and straightforward. When I left Tampa I knew I had lots of reading and hands-on experiences to gain to fully understand how the commercial fishing industry operated so my arguments would be factual.

That early lesson dealing with a militant outdoor writer was helpful during another "who gets the fish" controversy. Later on in this ongoing battle I met a young writer named Jeff Klinkenberg who wrote for the *St. Petersburg Times.* Mr. Klinkenberg leaned toward sport fishing, but he differed from other outdoor writers because he usually asked spokesmen from both sides of a fishing controversy to comment so his readers would read news and not propaganda.

A campaign designating speckled trout, red drum, king mackerel and Spanish mackerel as game fish was launched by the same groups who wanted all the fish for their constituents. In Florida, game fish cannot be sold. Therefore only anglers could enjoy species of fish designated as game fish. The game fish campaign prevented non-boaters, tourists or poor-people from eating the "game fish" designated fish unless they bought a boat, motor, trailer, bait, beer and license and went sport fishing.

The talking point of the day said limiting the fish to anglers was fair because everyone has a right to buy a boat, motor and trailer and go fishing. It is like saying driving on the interstate highway is limited to people driving a Mercedes because all citizens can buy a Mercedes and drive on the Interstate highway. Several legislators bought their argument.

The militant outdoors writers and angler lobbyists coerced Representative Dale Patchett (R) Vero Beach to file a bill every year designating red drum, speckled trout, king mackerel and Spanish mackerel as game fish. Every year Jerry Sansom, Executive Director of the Organized Fishermen of Florida, and I killed the Patchett bill because it was so appalling and greedy. The only species that received game-fish status decades later was red drum and the anglers paid a high price for stealing red drum for themselves.

After Herb Allen left the Tampa Tribune, he was followed by Frank Sergeant who took vitriolic comments against commercial fishing to a higher level. The Tampa Tribune always had outdoor writers banging on commercial fishermen, but the Tampa Tribune editorial board was one of the few newspapers that opposed the Florida net ban. The number of anti-commercial fishing writers has diminished since the commercial fishing industry was savaged by the net ban. So has the number of commercial fishing families. My original meeting with a radical element of the outdoor writers' profession opened my eyes on how mean-spirited their anti-commercial fishing campaigns would become.

CHAPTER 16

Bob Ingle and the St. Petersburg Lab

BOB INGLE WAS THE MOST SIGNIFICANT MARINE SCIENTIST I HAVE EVER MET. I was fortunate, or it was in my karma, to meet him in 1950 in St. Augustine when he worked for the Board of Conservation and busy building the Florida Marine Research Lab in St. Petersburg.

He was a ruggedly handsome, robust giant of a man with a deep-booming voice and full head of hair. He treasured every aspect of life and willingly accepted the joys and pain it brought his way. He was the kind of a man you wanted to be next to if a fight broke out at any watering hole frequented by men of the sea throughout the coastal villages of Florida. He was also the kind of a man you could ride from Tallahassee to Key West with and never be bored by conversation or weary from his sage advice.

Ingle stood six-foot-two with a slim waist in his early years and wide shoulders. He lit up a room full of people with his wit and wisdom and like many good men I've known, always took time to speak to everyone in the room, especially the ladies. He was totally comfortable with his feminine side. He treated everyone with respect if they let him.

Gary Usina, Sr., my brother-in-law, is a wise old man

who, from his experiences of loaning millions of dollars as a top banker in Florida, knows how people's minds work. We were talking about Bob Ingle one day and he said, "Bob had a glint in his eye and a set to his lips that often conveyed an unspoken 'I hope you are enjoying this conversation as much as I am'." Not everyone can put another person in that kind of moment.

In 1951, Bob was in charge of the Oyster Lab in Apalachicola. He'd been with the Board of Conservation nearly three years and was pushing the system as hard as he could for more funds to utilize and protect the prolific oyster bars in the nutrient-rich, shallow waters of Apalachicola Bay. There were over five-hundred oystermen working the beds in 1951 according to anecdotal information.

In 1957, the Board of Conservation established a marine research lab at Bayboro Harbor in St. Petersburg. Ingle was appointed Director. He and his staff of ten laid the groundwork for today's world-class research institute.

Llyn French tells the story of a young biologist who was walking down a corridor in Building C and saw Ingle coming his way. In a narrow corridor there was no way to avoid a close encounter with the big man. The Boss had a glare on his face.

""I hate you!" Ingle said.

"W-w-w-why?" stammered the newcomer, kneecaps rattling.

"Because," he burst into a laugh, "You're so skinny, and I'm so fat." There was a feeling of togetherness and an odd sort of happiness among the people fortunate to have worked under Bob Ingle.

When Ingle was working on a project at the lab or at sea on the *R/V Hernan Cortez*, he was all business. When he let his hair down after work, it was time for those who were present to hang on for whatever the night would bring. In his youth, and even in the 1950's and beyond, he carried himself like a steel-worker from Danville, Illinois, his hometown. He had a determined walk, sort of like John Wayne, but without the sideway saunter.

In his later years he resembled Ernest Hemingway with his conspicuous belly, whiskers, sometimes trimmed by a barber, and his thinning white hair that always looked windblown. He favored Hemingway's appearance, but had more knowledge about sea-critters than Hemingway could even imagine.

Llyn French, who knew Ingle and many people who worked with him, wrote me the following: "Bob hated dredge and fill. He loved Hemingway, anything Cuban, wild Florida, interesting people, dedicated hearts and this marine lab." She continued, "Whether you knew him or not, your career at FMRI was made possible by his untiring devotion. Carry it on."

One of the people Ingle hired and tutored was Bill Lyons. After Lyons was hired in 1964, he spent a few weeks of orientation in St. Petersburg and then was sent to the east coast field station. Not long afterwards, when he learned the lay of the land, he was assigned to the Caymans on a special lobster project. The trip was originally scheduled for three weeks, but because of problems getting lab gear to the site, he was there four months.

Ingle visited Lyons while he was working in the Cayman's and was impressed with his work. Ingle told him there was a job for him in St. Petersburg when he finished his Cayman assignment. He also told him he could finish his college education while working at the lab.

Lyons went back to college, earned his degree and then spent thirty-five years at the St. Petersburg lab. The many good years far outweighed a few tough ones caused by a shift in public policy toward the role of science in managing fisheries resources.

Lyons wrote a heartfelt letter to the Ingle family after Bob crossed over to the oyster bar in the sky, where the oysters are always plump and there's no angst within the oyster industry. He further wrote, " The lab was a place of excitement, of adventure, where we were thrilled to have opportunities to explore, learn and contribute. Bob led us, encouraged us, taught us, fed us when necessary, and chewed us out when we needed it. His faith in us was evident, and our loyalty to him absolute."

Ingle and his dedicated staff established an honest and efficient marine laboratory for the State of Florida. He started the lab with a minimum amount of funds and fought for every dollar the lab ever received. His contributions to science have been mostly unsung except by the men and women he touched and taught during his long and productive career.

He was tough...but caring. He had a quick and strong

temper...but the patience to work with people he believed in. He had the faraway look of a dreamer as well as the hard eyes of a master builder. He was complex, complicated and cantankerous. I loved him.

I became one of his special projects because he understood commercial fishermen and because he held the Usina family, my beloved in-laws, in great esteem. We trusted and respected each other from the moment we met on an old cypress dock at Palmo Cove located on the St. Johns River. He was someone I liked in 1950. How lucky for me to have him as my mentor starting in 1964. He was determined to teach me scientific stuff. I thought it was far above my ability to understand or assimilate, but I welcomed his patient tutelage.

He taught me how the scientific method works, and if I learned nothing else, I learned that well.

I get angry when I suspect conclusions of a scientific project are pre-determined before the hypothesis is tested and replications are completed. Science must be open and honest when it's put on the table so government managers who change or adopt new public policy have a sound basis for decisions.

For a scientist to use flawed data and trumped up statistics to accomplish a personal agenda is denigrating to the scientific profession as it hurts everyone. After a marine scientific research project is completed, but before it is published, it must be peer reviewed. An honest peer review makes it difficult for politicians and special interest groups to manipulate the conclusions to their own advantage.

It's very difficult for scalawags to manipulate scientific data if it is open to the public and available for honest comment. It was impossible to manipulate the science published by the St. Petersburg lab under Bob Ingle and his staff of honest biologists. Hopefully that will always be the case.

Ingle was proud of the Research Vessel, *Hernan Cortez,* a 73-foot wooden shrimp boat he used for exploratory fishing and scientific projects such as the hour-glass survey. The shrimp vessel was donated to the marine lab by L.C. Ringhaver, founder of Diesel Engine Sales, and a past president of the Southeastern Fisheries Association.

Ingle always gave me a hard stare when I referred to it as the <u>Herman</u> Cortez...he corrected me with great gusto saying, <u>Hernan</u> Cortez...<u>Hernan,</u> not <u>Herman.</u> I loved the way he said **Hernan** *with eyes blazing.* Sometimes I thought I heard steam hissing from his ears, but then he would smile at me and calm down because he knew I got to him again.

I met many professional scientists who worked for Bob Ingle, but knew Ed Joyce, Dale Beaumariage, Charlie Futch, Karen Steidinger, Vi Stewart, Bonnie Eldred and Ken Woodburn the best. Ed Joyce had St. Augustine connections. Joyce worked diligently on east coast shrimp biology and stock assessment in the early part of his career. Dale Beaumariage was working on pelagics and given the assignment to determine how many dead king mackerel fall to the ocean floor from gillnets.

Beaumariage is a man of great integrity. His scientific report did not support the claims of the angler groups so he was personally vilified in the press and by vicious political tactics.

This controversy lingers in my mind more than most because I saw honest science vilified by a radical sport fishing organization that dismisses all science that does not support its political goals.

Karen Steidinger was an early Ingle hire. She was one of the most dedicated employees Ingle and the lab ever had. I visited Karen in February, 2009, at the Florida Wildlife Research Institute, and asked her to share some of her feelings and thoughts about working with Bob Ingle for so many years.

"Bob Ingle created the lab and strived to keep it independent," Karen said as we began talking about the Ingle era.

Karen was working at a chemical lab in Connecticut, where she was ruiced, before migrating to Florida. She answered an advertisement in the *St. Petersburg Times* for a technician's job at the Florida Board of Conservation lab in 1963. She was interviewed by Bonnie Eldred, an outstanding person and dedicated scientist, who was one of the original biologists at the St. Pete Lab.

Karen was immediately hired by Bob Ingle. Based on Eldred's recommendation and his own innate ability to recognize talented people he felt he could push forward. I asked Karen what she thought when she first met Ingle. "He scared me at first," she said with a smile breaking across her face.

Karen earned her AA degree prior to taking the job, but Ingle told her she needed to go back to school and get her BS. "Get it in basket weaving, if you want", he said. "But get it." Of course she knew basket weaving meant get your degrees in scientific disciplines, not weaving a basket. Those who knew Ingle understood code words like basket weaving.

Ingle encouraged his employees to get a degree. Take time to go to school and then make it up the time lost later at the lab. For instance, it would take an hour drive from the lab to the USF campus in Tampa, one or two hours in class, and then an hour back to the lab----three days a week. The lost hours were always made up to make sure those that followed had the same opportunity. Karen wasn't the only lab technician or biologist who took advantage of the opportunity to finish college. She completed all her requirements and has been Dr. Karen Steidinger for decades.

I asked Karen to give me a one-word description of Bob Ingle.

"Magnificent," she said quickly and without batting an eye.

"He was like a second father. He paid more attention to me than my father."

"What else," I asked her.

"He was a friend – mentor – boss –smart – visionary and had faith in people."

She said that after she had been working at the lab for a month or so, Ingle told her to write an article on phytoplankton to use in the Lab's Leaflet Series he had initiated.

She wrote the article and submitted it to him feeling pretty good about her efforts. Ingle called her into his office a day or so later and told her it was good to have another person on the staff who could write and mentioned how helpful it would be in a variety of ways. He thanked her for her work then handed her article back.

"The whole article was in red ink except maybe for one sentence," Karen said, making the point that Ingle was a hard taskmaster, but a caring one.

Karen said the years under Ingle's tutelage passed too quickly. There was great opportunity for growth in the scientific profession. For employees who looked to learn something new, or seek the answer to some long-held hypothesis, the St. Petersburg lab was the place to be during Ingle era.

In old Building C, the hub of all activity for so many of the early years, there was a sign that said, "Communicate" as you walked down the hall and "Never Assume Anything" as you walked back up the hall. That was Ingle's philosophy.

Ingle knew reading was mandatory for learning. He read everything he could get his hands on and would sometimes ask a staff member if they had read such and such. When they said no he would usually hand them a copy. He was a visionary and a keeper of the flame.

Because he had a specific mental picture concerning the importance of west Florida's continental shelf, he and his staff designed the famous Hourglass Survey to test for benthic communities, fishery resources, plankton and currents. It was a twenty-eight month program confined to a geographical area from offshore Tampa Bay to Charlotte Harbor out to 73.2 meters depth.

The hourglass program released over 4,000 drift-bottles in conjunction with tracking red tide movements. Some bottles were returned from Mexico and some from North Carolina. In 1987, twenty years after the hourglass project ended, there was a red tide outbreak in North Carolina proving Gulf currents go all the way to North Carolina. This was an hourglass finding not believed by some scientists on the east coast. It was exciting to have a scientific conclusion validated. However, not all lab work was fun and rewarding.

Karen remembers one particular stressful incident when she and Charlie Futch recommended closure of Apalachicola Bay because of high counts of fecal coli form which happens naturally after heavy rains. The oyster industry was in an uproar because they could not harvest oysters if the bay was closed.

During this hullabaloo between the state lab and the oyster industry, an FSU professor told the press and oyster industry the river water was fresh and floated on top of the saltwater in the bay, so it couldn't get to the bottom and pollute the oysters. Consequently, he concluded that the oysters were okay even if the coli form counts were above the allowable level within the water column above the water on the bottom.

His conclusions were in error and were proved so later on, but his foray created severe animosity toward the two state biologists who were just doing their job. The Department of Natural Resources' (DNR) science indicated Apalachicola Bay was a predominately shallow estuary and therefore it was determined to be a total mixing zone. DNR correctly concluded the river water did in fact reach the bottom of the bay and did infect the oysters.

Karen and co-scientist Charlie Futch received death threats because of their scientific recommendation to close the bay to oyster harvesting. Karen was called late at night and the caller threatened to cut her up and throw her in the bay. It was probably whisky-talking by a bully, but that kind of intimidation makes it tougher for concerned scientists who want to help fishermen.

DNR brought in an expert hydrology professor from the University of Florida who proved beyond a shadow of a doubt that the river water did penetrate to the bottom of the bay and affected oyster meat. The U of F report stopped the controversy. The good science done by dedicated state workers turned out to be correct after all the hate-filled rhetoric and a death threat.

In the early days of the Ingle era, state lab technicians earned a whopping $300 per month. On many occasions, near the end of the month when everyone was almost broke, the biologists and technicians had very little food in their larders. One enjoyable method of survival was for everyone to pitch in their loose coins and prepare a community spaghetti dinner. This allowed the grossly-underpaid lab technicians to enjoy a home-cooked meal at a price they could afford.

Those survival meals, as the staff called them, created a venue to have open and frank discussions about
scientific projects planned or underway at the lab. This
fortuitous gathering of such intelligent people working
under Bob Ingle forged lifetime bonds sustaining them
through good times and bad times at Camelot on the
Bay.

Ed Joyce, one of Ingle's finest protégés, loyal friend
and employee, was appointed lab director when Ingle retired. A trio of achievers and professionals followed Joyce
in the lab director's slot. They were Dale Beaumariage,
then Fred Kalber, then Karen Steidinger. These dedicated
scientists learned much of their craft and much more
about life from Bob Ingle.

Ingle died in 1997, just before Karen's mother passed
away. I asked Karen how she felt when she heard of
Ingle's death.

"Very, very sad....personal loss worse than when my
father died. Bob Ingle always encouraged me and wanted
me to succeed."

What else crossed your mind?" I asked.

"One of the saddest things was not knowing what
happened to Robin, Ingle's daughter whom he loved so
much and wanted to be closer," she said with a tear
welling up.

Karen and I stopped talking after sharing good
thoughts about Robin. We spent another hour of quality
time perusing old photos of the original lab personnel and
the ones who stayed through the 1980's.

We were in the moment and said so. We delighted

in creating a passageway through the mirror of time to once again glimpse how very young, strong, energetic and naïve we were. It was a memorable visit with a wonderful lady. I told her I was going to find Bob's children and talk to them.

Ingle's middle son Charlie and I had a breakfast meeting at the Village Inn in Tallahassee a few days after I returned home. I hadn't seen him in years. When I called and asked him to talk to me about his dad he sounded excited.

I first met Charlie when he was fifteen years old living with his parents on Mission Road in Tallahassee, but he doesn't recall the meeting. He doesn't look much different than he did twenty years ago, except there's a modest amount of gray hair that was once dark. He is still slim and his pleasant smile lights up a room just like his dad's. He is cerebral and has the skill to build anything a person can think of or design. His unique craftsmanship is without peer.

His first recollection of me was in the fall of 1966 when I built a fireplace for his dad at their rustic cabin on the high banks of the Ochlocknee River. He remembers helping me, but I wouldn't let him carry bricks or bring mortar up the ladder to the mortar board sitting on the scaffold. My arrangement with his daddy was I would build the fireplace, but he had to serve as my hod carrier and mortar mixer. I wanted him to feel the pain. I wanted him to feel what it was like not being the boss.

I loved hollering for mud and bricks and listening to old Ingle grumbling, even though he grumbled with happiness in his low voice. I almost made him humble on several days when I worked him especially hard, but he never quit. I asked Charlie to tell me the first thing he remembers about his dad.

Charlie was born in Apalachicola in 1949 and remembered an incident when he was four years old. He said he remembers his older brother Bobby falling out of a tree in their front yard and landing hard on his back. Daddy Ingle ran out of the house and knelt over Bobby and told him to lie still. He thought Bobby might have broken his back so he ran back in the house and called Dr. Fotis Nichols, local doctor and a local icon.

Charlie remembers Nichols driving up to their house in his snazzy convertible with the top down and breeze blowing through the doctor's thinning hair. He stepped from the car to assess the situation. He and Daddy Ingle decided they needed a plank to strap Bobby on so his back would not be injured any further. They found a wide cypress board under the porch and strapped Bobby on it using belts and rope.

There wasn't any ambulance service so they gently picked Bobby up and placed the boy on the board on the passenger side of the convertible. Bobby's head stuck high above the windshield as they drove through town to the hospital. Charlie said that's a sight he can never forget. I told him I doubted anyone could forget such a moment.

He told me the first outing he remembers was his

dad taking the family way up the Apalachicola River. He remembered riding in a Board of Conservation boat. They took a picnic lunch and he enjoyed watching his dad study the river and its critters. Charlie knew he was a scientist and was probably looking for signs concerning the health of the river and any indications the water was better or worse than usual.

Charlie described his dad as a giant of a man, in height and strength and character. By the time Charlie was in high school he knew his dad had a restless curiosity and a scientific bent towards anything. It wasn't enough for him to hear about something being one way or the other; he wanted to know if the person arrived at his conclusion using the scientific method. Like other world-class scientists he was always searching. He epitomized the cliché, "The more I learn the less I know."

Charlie said he thinks of his parents daily and sees them in so many different ways. He especially thinks of his dad when he is on the land by the Ochlooknee River, land loved so much by his dad.

Before we shook hands and I headed to my office to copy a picture of Ingle and a dock full of sturgeon I asked him, "If your dad was here today, sitting here with us in this restaurant at this moment, what would you tell him?" Charlie's eyes became a little moist when they met mine. With that special Ingle grin he said he would tell him, "Thanks for everything. I wish I would have known then what I know now."

Then I asked Charlie what he admired most about his dad and he said, "Everything—his loyalty." When I asked what his dad taught him about life, he reflected again for a moment then looked at me with that big Ingle grin and said, "Shakespeare—To thine own self be true." I told him that was very revealing for it's a classic way to say "be truthful in all things". The rest of that verse from Hamlet says, "And it must follow, as the night and day. Thou canst not then be false to any man."

CHAPTER 17

Senator Randolph Hodges – A good man

IN THE LATE 1960'S, I MET CONGRESSMAN BOB SIKES OF CRESTVIEW, FLORIDA ON A HUNTING TRIP AT SENATOR RANDOLPH HODGES' BEAR CREEK FARM IN GADSDEN COUNTY NOT FAR FROM THE TOWN OF MIDWAY. Hodges and Sikes were longtime legislative friends and Florida icons. Hodges was a former state senator from Cedar Key and served as Senate President in 1961. After retiring from the Senate, the governor and cabinet selected him to be the Executive Director of the Florida Board of Conservation.

The Hodges family owned a seafood packing facility and ice-house in Cedar Key for decades. Several members of his family were commercial mullet and crab fishermen so he had great knowledge of the Florida seafood industry and the laws regulating the industry.

Congressman Sikes and Hodges were active political leaders during the heyday of the "Pork-chop Gang," composed of north Florida legislators. These rural oriented men ruled the state for decades under the provisions of the 1868 Florida Constitution adopted after the War Between the States.

The term "Pork Chop Gang" is attributed to James

Clendenin in an editorial he wrote for the *Tampa Tribune* in 1955. Earlier references tying pork chops to North Florida legislators can be found in numerous Florida archives and old newspapers. The Pork Chop Gang ran Florida until the U.S. Supreme Court's "One-Man-One Vote" decision in 1962 that forced a complete redistricting of legislative districts in all states.

The Supreme Court's decision transferred political power and control of tax money from North Florida to Central and South Florida where the majority of residents and voters lived. As a novice lobbyist, focused only on commercial fishing and the seafood industry, I didn't know much about the Pork Chop Gang. All I knew was the North Florida legislators I worked with supported commercial fishing, the Florida seafood industry and treated us with respect.

Sikes served in the Florida legislature before launching a nineteen-term career in the U.S. House of Representatives which ended on January 3, 1979. Sikes was known far and wide as the "he coon." The definition of a he-coon varies. Former Florida governor Lawton Chiles was quoted in the *St. Petersburg Times* as saying "The old he-coon walks just before the light of day." He may also have said the he-coon is the oldest and strongest of the litter. Whatever the correct definition, my experiences with men who earned that label were that they were warm-hearted, very wise politicians who knew what made people tick and knew how to use their fleeting power to the fullest. Hodges, Sikes and Chiles were all he-coons in my life.

SENATOR RANDOLPH HODGES – A GOOD MAN

This story isn't about political power or walking late at night or early in the morning. It's about a young man from St. Augustine who never hunted until he was married and honorably discharged from the Marine Corps. I never imagined when I was on a scaffold laying a brick wall or pouring concrete in late August at St. Augustine Beach with the sun burning my tanned skin darker every day that I would be friends with two Florida political icons who treated me with utmost kindness and respect.

On trips to Washington D.C. to lobby for funding of the Board of Conservation research and marketing projects, Randolph Hodges, Harmon Shields and I went to Congressman Sikes office as soon as we arrived at the Capitol. I always brought a cooler full of boiled shrimp, crab meat, smoked Spanish mackerel and stone crabs. We were very popular and always welcomed by the Florida delegation.

PL 88-309 is a law authorizing the U.S. Department of Agriculture to collect tariffs on fishery products exported to the United States. Agriculture keeps most of the funds which I never understood, but we could not pry one dime from those tight fists at Ag A small portion of the tariff went to the Bureau of Commercial Fisheries which was housed in the Department of Interior at that time. The Bureau was later transferred to the Department of Commerce.

Bob Sikes was the leader of the Florida delegation that was composed of ten Democrats and two Republicans in 1965. The Republicans were Ed Gurney and Bill Cramer. Congressman Sikes office secured a one-time one million dollar appropriation earmarked for the U.S. Bureau of Commercial Fisheries to promote domestic shrimp nationwide. I testified before the House Appropriations Committee and was treated with kindness by the Chairman who was a close friend of Sikes. Sikes was Subcommittee Chairman for Military Construction. Sikes loved Florida and supported commercial fishermen and all workers in Florida.

Flying back from one of those successful congressional visits, Hodges invited me to his Bear Creek farm the next time Congressman Sikes came over from Crestview for a deer and bird hunt. Sure enough, the Congressman came down later in the month and Hodges asked me to come to the farm and bring a big bowl of large St. Augustine shrimp if they were available. They were always available in those days for lobbying.

When I arrived at the cook shack and got out of my car, Hodges knew by the look of my clothes and my lack of a hat that I wasn't much of a hunter, but he insisted I participate in the afternoon deer hunt. I eagerly accepted, even though I didn't have any camo clothes. I wore a heavy blue windbreaker, red flannel shirt and a pair of old USMC work pants with baggy pockets in the front instead of on the side. As George Goble once said on the Johnny Carson show, "Have you ever felt like the world was a tuxedo and you were a pair of brown shoes?" I was definitely a brown, unpolished pair of shoes with broken shoestrings.

The other guests, all of whom were active and high-up in Florida politics, looked like they stepped out of an outfitter's store in Atlanta or Birmingham. They wore camo hats and camo boots and carried camo gun cases. I wondered if they were wearing camo underwear, but I didn't dare ask any of them because I was the youngest man at the camp. I was the token whippersnapper.

It was late-afternoon and time to stake out our hunting stands so I walked over to my car and waited for Hodges to show me where I would be hunting. I heard some of the older men talking about the covered stand at the creek. They also talked about the stand where corn had grown during the summer and early fall saying it was lying on the ground, rotting. I didn't hear anyone say they would hunt over a baited field so that was good. Even as a rookie hunter I knew that was illegal.

"Get in your car, Bob, and follow me," Randolph said as he picked up his rifle and headed for his black Falcon pickup truck.

"Lead on Senator," I replied.

We drove along a grass road near several stands of cypress for ten or fifteen minutes then came to a big open-field surrounded on three sides by a hardwood forest and high grass. I stepped out of my white Plymouth Fury III and walked over to Hodges. He had his window down and said, "Back up close to that tall grass and watch for deer to run or walk out of the woods. Listen to the dogs to figure out where they are and I'll check back with you later on," he said, and then drove away to wherever his stand was located.

I figured he didn't have to be too far away because all I had was a 16 gauge Remington shotgun with three number one buckshot shells so chances of me hitting him were slim. He didn't give me specific hunting instructions figuring I knew all I needed to know about deer hunting. The deer would have to get close for me to get a shot using a 16 gauge Remington. If I had my old M-1 then I might hit one at 200 yards. The deer population would not be in jeopardy that cool, sunny day.

I backed my shiny, freshly-waxed white car into the grass and sat there for a long time watching the bright-blue sky, the swaying moss in the trees and appreciating the fact I was alive and on a real deer hunt. I never saw any deer or heard any dogs that were close, but enjoyed the afternoon hunting experience.

About ten minutes before dark, I saw Randolph's truck headed toward me. He stopped next to my open door on the passenger's side where I was relaxing.

"See any deer, Bob?' he asked.

"Not a one Senator", I reported.

He looked straight at me and the way I was set up for hunting. Then, in that good-old-boy Cedar Key drawl said, "Chances are purty good you won't see any deer as long as you smoke that big cigar and listen to old songs on your radio."

He had a twinkle in his eye that was a visual communication clearly telling me I just got my first lesson on deer hunting from a master.

"Follow me to the camp and we'll eat some of those giant shrimp Johnny Salvador sent."

After his crystal-clear observation I felt embarrassed. I immediately learned that hunting deer while puffing on an Optima cigar and listening to oldie Goldie's on the FM radio isn't the North Florida way to hunt deer, but nobody had ever explained the process to me before. I wondered what the real hunters would think about my hunting skills.

Hodges, always the gentleman, didn't say a word about my hunting expertise when we got back to camp. I got real busy getting the ten-count shrimp out of the cooler, concocting my famous pink sauce. I then stacked a pile of humongous St. Augustine white shrimp in a plastic bowl in the center of the over-size and well used cypress picnic table.

Thankfully the evening of good food, smooth whiskey and country-boy fellowship wasn't marred by exposing the antics of a rank amateur hunter. However, I often wondered if Hodges could restrain himself from telling the story of the great, one-of-a-kind, former Marine, St. Augustine deer slayer after I went home late that night. I'm not sure if there was any connection, but it was about five years before Hodges invited me on another deer hunt.

On my second deer hunt, Hodges gave me a map to his Gulf Hammock land in levy County so I knew when to pull through the open gate near the landmarks he had told me about. The map said drive across the cattle-guard and head west toward the woods until I see signs of a cabin or until somebody sees me if I get lost. I found the cabin with the help of the unmistakable sounds of a dozen Beagle hunting-dogs yapping in their pens.

I parked my Chevy station-wagon away from the cabin so I wouldn't interfere with any activities, picked up my duffel-bag and walked over to where Harmon Shields, Randolph Hodges and his son Gene were standing and shook their hands. Gene told me to put my goods inside the old-wooden cabin and find an empty cot or bed and make myself at home. There was a kitchen, bathroom and a spacious gathering-room for lots of folks to lie on the floor in their sleeping bags. It was rustic with deer heads, mounted wood ducks and turkey beards hanging on the walls.

Mike Hodges, Gene's son, and several other young boys from Cedar Key were outside messing with the dogs and looking at their guns. I don't recall what was cooking, but it could have been ribs, biscuits and gravy. It was about 2:00 PM and Randolph said we would be going to the deer stands in a couple of hours. I told Randolph I didn't own a rifle so he loaned me an over-under rifle to use. I'd never seen an over-under with a shotgun barrel on top and rifle barrel underneath or vice versa but figured it was just another weapon, so no problem.

At the appointed hour we piled into Randolph's truck and headed out into the deep-woods. There were numerous deer stands, some in trees, some stand alones that were only for skinny people and some that were a piece of plywood laying on top of four 4″ X 4″ posts with no sides, rails or anything - just a flat, unpainted, weathered piece of plywood. Harmon Shields and Gene Hodges had their favorite stands so they were dropped off first. I was the last one Randolph dropped off before he went to his special stand. We traveled about two miles down a long straight road with high bushes and pine, oak and cypress trees on both sides until we came to a small clearing.

"Okay, Bob," Randolph said. "Here's your gun and bullets. Watch out for the second step on the ladder. We had a legislator fall off it last week and we haven't had time to fix it."

"Don't worry. My 200 pounds won't hit the ground if I can help it," I said as I took the gun and headed toward the deer stand with the unstable wooden ladder.

I examined the broken step and knew I couldn't use it. The third one looked solid so did the rest all the way up the twelve foot ladder. The gun didn't have a sling so I clutched it in my right hand, put the bullets in my jacket pocket and started up. I kept my boots to the outside of each step where the wood was strongest. I made it to the top without incident. Upon reaching the platform, I immediately discovered my home for the next few hours had bird poop all over it and I didn't have anything to push it aside except my Elmer Fudd type hunting cap. That hunting cap was washed several times after I got home, but was subsequently recycled by the trash truck.

Randolph gave me three rifle bullets and three shot-gun shells. I did not think I would get many chances to shoot with a single-shot borrowed gun. On top of that he gave me the wrong gauge shotgun shells. I had three rifle bullets. I felt better than Barney Fife felt when Sheriff Andy Taylor gave him a gun without bullets, but not by much.

A CULTURE WORTH SAVING

It was a beautiful North Florida wintry day. Bright sunshine with few clouds meant the weather forecast for falling temperature would probably be true. There were large cypress trees near me, ones that escaped the efforts of the carpetbaggers who ravaged most Florida forests following the Civil War. They destroyed virgin forests without reservation to make pencils and building materials for the North.

After I settled down and was quiet for a few minutes the forest came alive with a cacophony of sound. I have found that time spent listening to critters in a great forest is magical. Time passes too quickly when body and soul are in the process of being rejuvenated.

Observing a wild animal materialize near the edge of a forest is mystical. One minute you are sitting still and quiet, nothing moving except your eyes scanning the panorama at the forest's edge. The next moment an un-mistakable profile of a wild deer appears out of nowhere. That's exactly what happened when I was sitting on that plywood platform - twelve-feet off the ground - in Gulf Hammock. A beautiful deer stood in my line of sight and stood as still as a statue.

It was getting dark and the wind was picking up. I had to make certain it was a buck because Randolph told us not to shoot a doe. I had mixed emotions as my eyes strained to identify the deer – would it be a doe or would it be a buck - and would I kill it or miss with a rifle I never shot before? It felt a bit like the first time I qualified on the firing line in Parris Island many years before.

I watched the splendid critter stand motionless for

what seemed like an eternity but was only a matter of minutes. When it bent down to feed on the grass I saw the spike. I eased the rifle to my shoulder, took aim down the barrel and lined up the hard-sight for what I knew would be my only shot. I gently squeezed the trigger. The buck fell at the same time I heard the sound of the rifle. The head shot killed the deer instantly. I didn't feel as elated as I thought I would and that was the last deer I ever killed. I shoot them now with a camera.

I ejected the round and slipped another one in the chamber. I concentrated my eyes on the same area in case a big buck appeared. None did and that was fine with me. It was totally dark fifteen minutes later.

It was time to come down the rickety-ladder without benefit of sunlight. I slid my legs off the platform trying to avold the bird doo. My big boot felt the second step and I descended safely to the ground. I walked fitty yards to the deer, grabbed him by the spike and front legs and pulled him across the open-field toward the dirt road leading to the cabin.

My heart was beating hard, probably more from the quick descent down the ladder and pulling the deer across the grass field than from the adrenalin rush you get when hunting wild game. I made it to the road, leaving the deer a few yards back so the truck or ATV I hoped for would come soon and could turn around. I had a small flashlight attached to my jacket and two oranges in the pockets. The oranges tasted like nectar of the gods.

Ten minutes passed without seeing headlights or hearing the sound of a car headed my way. It was pitch-black, no moon and I wondered if this was an area of Gulf Hammock where snakes, alligators, wildcats, coyotes and bears came out at night in search of food. Would predators be interested in me or in the fresh-killed deer laying a few yards away?

The mind is a scary place to go by yourself in the middle of Gulf Hammock or sometimes even in the safety of your home. I wondered if leaving me deep in the woods with no idea which way back to the camp was part of the ritual for Tallahassee hunting rookies. I muttered to myself, "If this is part of the routine, then this good old country-boy will never come back to Gulf Hammock." I was too old for this stuff. I was getting angry and about to walk down the road to somewhere.

Moments before I started walking, I heard the distinct sound of a one-cylinder All-Terrain-Vehicle, and then saw the headlight flickering up and down among the bushes and trees as it bounced along the road. My tension subsided considerably. The man on the ATV was a friend of the Hodges who I hadn't met before. He was a big, strong boy you wanted as a friend in a tough situation.

"How'd you do?" he gruffly asked.

"Okay," I said just as gruff.

"I heard a shot... sounded like it came from your stand. Did you see something?"

"Yep, shot a spike and he's lying over there," I said with a touch of pride in my voice.

I thought the big man was going to choke from surprise. He leapt off the ATV, turned on his powerful flashlight and walked over to the deer. He grabbed the spike. He walked back and said,

"It's a spike; nice size too. You got the only kill. Mr. Randolph will be happy."

"Surprised may be a better word," I murmured real low.

"Hop on," he said. I'll take you back to camp then get the deer afterwards."

"Sounds good to me," I said in my nicest voice. "I sure am hungry."

Two things came to mind as I climbed on the soft, wide seat of the Honda ATV. First, I was thankful to be sitting on an ATV, leaving the dark-woods of Gulf Hammock which can swallow man or beast. Secondly was my awareness that Senator Randolph Hodges will know better than anyone I wasn't chomping on a cigar and listening to music this time. I was hunting like a family member and was the only one who brought venison back to camp.

A country feast prepared in the middle of Gulf Hammock is an experience anyone who likes good food should do at least once. The repartee, jokes and hunting experiences told in true redneck fashion were better than being at the Comedy Zone. The drive back to Tallahassee early the next morning was enjoyable and I looked forward to frying the big piece of back strap they awarded me for Mindy and the kids.

CHAPTER 18

A Charter Boat Captain

"DAMN YOU BOB JONES FOR TAKING OFF MY BLINDERS," CAPTAIN B. J."PUT" PUTNAM SAID ON OUR WAY BACK TO FLORIDA FROM A GULF COUNCIL MEETING.

"I didn't take off your blinders, Put, you snatched them off yourself when you saw the real catch records for king mackerel," I responded.

I knew Captain Put could see the grin on my face in the rear view mirror of the Dodge Van. He and O.B. Lee were playing gin rummy on the console between two captain-chairs. I was the designated driver for the trip back to Florida from New Orleans.

As Gulf of Mexico Fisheries Management Council members we voted on allocation of the king mackerel harvest between commercial and recreational fishermen. Many sport magazines had written how the commercial fishermen were devastating the king mackerel by catching the majority of them. Those of us in the industry knew we were catching far less than the anglers, but nobody would listen to us, much less believe what we were telling them for years.

When the federal government's king mackerel stock assessment showed anglers caught 70% of the king mackerel in the Gulf of Mexico and commercial fishermen caught 30%, they demanded that their share of fish be determined by their past harvests. The anglers finally believed what we had been telling them because anglers caught 70% of the king mackerel and the commercial fishermen caught 30%. The anglers were happy about the king mackerel allocation because they got most of the fish. Unfortunately, they don't like the process when historical landings show the commercial catch has historically been higher than the anglers catch. If they get most of the fish they are happy, but if the consumers get the most through a commercial harvest, they are usually angry and petulant.

When Congress passed the Magnuson-Stevens Fisheries Conservation and Management Act they established a 200-mile federal fishing zone and regional fishery management councils to implement the law. I was appointed to the Gulf of Mexico Fishery Management Council as the commercial fishing representative, B.J. Putnam was appointed the recreational representative and Harmon Shields was designated by Senator Randolph Hodges as the council member representing Florida's marine resource agency.

I had never met Capt. Putnam but felt he must be a good guy if he was from Panama City or he wouldn't have been appointed on Senator Hodges recommendation to Governor Reuben Askew. Harmon told me I ought to meet Capt. Putnam so he and I drove to Panama City.

Capt. Putnam was sitting in a booth at a local restaurant with other charter boat owners when Harmon and I walked in. When he saw Harmon he came over. Harmon introduced us. We had a long handshake with both of us exerting a little extra pressure on each other's hand. Neither of us flinched nor felt any pain from the handshake. It was like two silverbacks meeting on a jungle path as we both tipped the scale well over two-hundred and thirty pounds.

"I've heard about you," Capt. Put said.

"Hope everything wasn't all bad," I replied.

"We will have difference of opinions on the Council and I want you to know I'll fight for what I believe," he told me looking straight in my eyes.

"I wouldn't expect anything less." I said. "You know I'll be doing the same thing."

He nodded his head and that was the driving force of our first meeting. He told me a little bit about his background as a charter boat owner and how he took his boat, *Lady M,* to the Keys in the winter time when the weather was bad in Panama City.

I gave him my background including the fact I had been working for Southeastern Fisheries Association for twelve years and had served on numerous fishery committees at the state and federal level. I told him about our distant-water commercial fishing boats fishing off Mexico and other Central American countries.

I told him we knew years ago that if the United States adopted a 200-mile fishing zone all nations would follow suit. When foreign countries established their exclusive fishing zones our distant water fleets were forced to return to the Gulf of Mexico and the South Atlantic Ocean. I told him that was one of the reasons my association opposed the Magnuson Act, but our biggest concern was what would happen to Florida commercial fisheries when the federal government assumed total control of the fisheries.

He was not as concerned as I was because he didn't think the federal government would ever bother the recreational fishing industry because of so many little boats that only caught a few fish.

At the time charter boats considered themselves as recreational fishermen, though I always considered them commercial along with anyone else who made money from fishing. We had some interesting and testy discussions on this point in the beginning of our relationship, until he removed his blinders and, at the same time, I came up the learning curve on what makes a charter boat owner/captain tick.

One of our best friends was Carl Anderson of the legendary Panama City Anderson fishing family. Carl had a charter boat, a wholesale/retail seafood business and other entrepreneurial ventures. Carl, Putnam and I became golfing buddies and played whenever I came to Panama City. Captain Carl was a solid citizen with a good feel for the mood of the people. He was honest and personable in all dealings with the association and all segments of the Florida fishing industry. Carl Anderson served over twenty-five years on the Southeastern Fisheries Association's Board of Directors. He was a giver, not a taker. The Anderson's are icons in the charter and party boat industry. Carl gave Captain Put and I much good advice as did Captain Buster Niquet. Captain Billy Archer, owner of the Charter boat *Seminole Wind,* is a lot like Captain Put.

Captain Put loved music and could easily name songs going back to the 1940s. In most cases he knew a verse or two. We often checked each other out by humming a tune and then asking for the name of the song. I always chuckled when we played "Name that Tune" especially if there was anyone else around listening to two, rather large, bearded good 'ol boys, humming songs made popular by Bing Crosby or Frank Sinatra or even unknown singers.

Captain Put lived life with several passions. You never had to guess how he felt about an issue because his face would turn a deep red and he might get a little puffy jawed if he thought what was being said was heifer dust. When this happened it was best to stand a few feet back when he began speaking.

Captain Put was the most adamant, hardcore, belligerent, cantankerous, dedicated Alabama Crimson Tide football fan I have ever known. There were a couple of things you did not want to do to Capt. Put unless you were ready to fight. One was to show disrespect for Bear Bryant or anything relating to the University of Alabama and the other was to scare him with a snake.

Two vivid snake incidents come to mind. The first one he told me about was once while he was getting a haircut and beard trim, the barber pulled a rubber snake out of a drawer and laid it on the arm of the Captain Put's chair.

Capt. Put was deathly afraid of snakes. I don't mean

a little bit scared, I mean he flat didn't like them and they frightened him almost to madness. When this incident occurred he leapt out of the chair, snatching the barber cloth off as he ran out the door, listening to the barber and everyone inside laughing.

He went home but returned to the barber shop in about fifteen minutes in a full rage. He walked quickly to the barber who had put the snake on his chair - just visualize a very big man with a scarlet red face - and pulled a loaded pistol out of his pants pocket and jammed it into the barber's mouth and asked him just one question. "Do you want to laugh at me now?" he said looking so deep in the man's eyes he could see his soul.

Capt. Put told me the barber turned white with fright and dampened his khaki pants. Capt. Put and I agreed that only through the intercession of God did he not pull the trigger.

"I bet that barber never scares anyone else with a rubber snake," I speculated one evening while we were playing gin rummy. Capt. Put got a faraway look in his eyes, but didn't say a word. I never mentioned this incident to him for the rest of his life.

The second incident happened in Tampa when we were playing a round of golf with Steve Cox on East Lake golf course which is laden with cypress trees and shallow dark water ponds, a perfect habitat for all kind of snakes especially water moccasins. As a native Floridian, I never venture into high grass near cypress ponds on a golf course without a golf club in my hand, staying alert for any movement on the ground or something round and black hanging from a limb.

We were on the back nine this glorious day. Unfortunately there were no restroom facilities anywhere in sight. As a man, when urinary relief is necessary on a golf course, you simply find a big tree and shield yourself from prying eyes playing the next hole.

Captain Put found a tree and was leisurely reducing bladder pressure when I noticed a fat water-moccasin about five feet from where he stood. The snake wasn't moving - just lying in the sun, almost camouflaged among the multi colored leaves.

Knowing how out of control Captain Put would get if I yelled, I first of all made sure what I saw was a real snake and not a branch because I didn't want him coming after me. I backed away a few more steps toward the cart and said in a very calm voice, "Captain Put, listen to me and do exactly what I tell you." I saw him flinch so I quickly said, "Just start backing up slowly toward me, okay?"

He started backing up and put his arms by his side. As he stepped back his "watering device" started fanning first to the left and then to the right. I got so tickled by what was happening I almost burst out laughing, but I held it in until he was back at the cart and sat down. He saw the snake so he knew I wasn't trying to fool him and then he saw me start laughing.

"What the hell's a matter with you?" he said with a bit of menace in his voice.

"I'm not laughing at the snake or your predicament that I walked you out of," I said. "I'm laughing at the way you backed up and watered the grass for four feet on either side like a precision made water sprinkler."

Thankfully, I had him laughing by the time we got to the 19th Hole for a drink and a snack. We talked about his snake encounter among the trees in Tampa many times and both of us always chuckled.

Capt. Put became an experienced, articulate and knowledgeable member of the Gulf of Mexico Fishery Management Council. He had vast knowledge about finding and catching billfish. He led the Gulf of Mexico Fishery Management Council's effort to secure tuna harvest records from a Japanese tuna boat fishing in the Gulf of Mexico.

The Council didn't have authority to manage tuna fishing because tuna were managed under an international treaty which established harvest levels. But, the Council wanted to know what was happening to the tuna resources in the Gulf of Mexico. The Council pushed Japan for historical and current fishing records until the Japanese government finally allowed an observer to come aboard a Japanese tuna boat that was fishing in the Gulf of Mexico.

The observer selected by the Council and approved by the Japanese officials was, of course, Captain Put. Even though he did not speak Japanese he gladly boarded the Japanese longline vessel at sea to observe a highly professional and efficient operation.

During the voyage he became friends with the

Japanese captain and crew. He respected them and they respected him. They realized he knew a great deal about billfish because he had studied their habits and their habitats for years.

In his report to the Gulf Council after the voyage, he said the interaction with the Japanese fishing captain and crew will always be one of his fondest memories. He saw how professional fishermen conducted themselves and how they followed strict handling procedures, maintaining the highest quality of the fish so valuable in Japan. His work on the Japanese longline vessel was also significant for future management. His work was important in building an administrative record based on accurate, observed data instead of assumptions or hearsay.

Capt. Put invited me to a billfish tournament one weekend so I packed my neatest togs and showed up at his house in Bay Point ready to go early the next morning. We boarded an absolutely gorgeous yacht owned by one of his friends who fished the big-money tournaments. I immediately climbed the ladder to the bridge where the big leather chairs were located to get some sun.

We got underway within an hour. When we reached dark blue water Capt. Put got the lures, teasers and all kinds of paraphernalia ready. Then, he put the lines out, clipping several to the outriggers. When everything was in place he came topside. He told me to watch the tip of the rods and call out if I saw any movement at all. I told him that would be easy enough for a grouper grabber to do.

This was my first billfish trip. I do not enjoy watching a feather or special wired-up ballyhoo bait flip-flop around on top of the waves all day long, waiting for some finicky billfish to hook itself. After two hours of boring trolling I put a cushion on the deck and stretched out on my back. I tilted my FSU cap forward to cover most of my eyes from direct sunlight and began watching the clouds to see if they formed an animal or some kind of recognizable image. I enjoy watching clouds on the bridge of a million dollar yacht. I glanced at the rods every now and then, but not often.

In about an hour, Captain Put came back up the ladder and asked if I had seen any action at all.

"Nope, haven't seen anything but one of the clouds looked a little bit like a monster I once saw in a movie," I said without looking at him.

"Are you watching the clouds?" he roared, his face turning purple. "Are you watching the damn clouds for God's sake?"

"Yep," I said.

"What in the hell are you watching the clouds for? You're supposed to be watching the tip of the rod and the action of the baits," he bellowed.

"Well, there wasn't any action on the damn poles so I'm looking at clouds," I said with a bit of amusement in my voice. I knew his face would be flushing a deeper shade of purple hardly ever seen.

He muttered something inaudible as he slid down the ladder with his feet on the outside rails. I'm glad I didn't hear exactly what he said because I'm using language fit for the entire family in this story and wouldn't like to quote the good Captain Put using blue language.

He never invited me back for another bill fishing trip. Actually, once was enough for me. Trying to hook a billfish is not nearly as exciting as hooking a 20-pound grouper on a rocky bottom or casting into schools of bait with a light rod and open face reel for king or Spanish mackerel, which I often did near Dog Island and Alligator Point.

We often talked about his early years learning the trade and his experiences while charter fishing in the Keys. We drove all over the Gulf region to fishery management council meetings so there was plenty of time to talk and bond.

One time he told me about bringing his boat home from the Keys after the season was over. I asked him if he stayed close to shore on the trip to Panama City.

"The shortest way home was a straight line from the Keys to the Panama City sea buoy," he said. "That's the course I set and I ran it without stopping."

"How did you stay awake? Were you by yourself," I asked.

"I was by myself and didn't want to spend any money at a marina or lose time getting home. It was hard as hell to keep my eyes open, but it's what I had to do," he said.

"Did you ever have any close calls?" I asked.

"I never had any close calls with other boats, but looking out the windshield on a totally dark night can play terrible tricks on your mind," he recalled.

"Such as?" I pressed.

"You see things that aren't real. Several times heading into a rough sea, I thought I would be swamped by rogue waves higher than a skyscraper that seemed absolutely real," he said. "I knew they weren't real, but had to struggle with my mind to keep the wheel steady and stay on compass. Sometimes I would just stare at the instruments. Eventually the imagined waves faded from my mind."

"That was a tough deal" I said in a low voice. "I know you're glad that phase of your life is over. "

"I don't miss that part of the Keys experience, but I miss the characters I met. There are some crazy folks down there who are the salt of the earth," he said. "Must be the margaritas making them act the way they do."

"There are crazy folks in Tallahassee and Panama City as well," I responded. "Maybe they're everywhere just so we can cross paths, visit for a little while, and then tell stories about each other."

Captain Put and I had six productive years together on the Gulf Council. We had a positive impact on the operation of the Council and the conservation of the marine resources. We established fair and transparent management protocols that lasted for many years.

I was not appointed to the Gulf Council for my third allowable term because I wouldn't change my party affiliation from Democrat to Republican. The fish I represented didn't belong to any party, but as often happens; politics ruined a well-designed and fair federal fishery management process.

Capt. Put was blessed with a loving wife and family. He and Fan had two boys and one girl, Tom, Richard and Stacey - good kids who bring much joy to the Putnam clan. Tommy is part-owner of Half-Hitch Tackle Shop in Panama City and Destin, Richard works as a free-lance boat captain, and Stacey teaches nursing at Gulf Coast College in Panama City. Fan's grandchildren are the pride of her life and she's always ready to show the latest pictures of her beautiful grandkids. Fan is a charming lady who is the epitome of a loving wife, mother and grandmother.

Captain Put and I stayed friends for the rest of his life, which was far too short. Several years before he passed, we drove to Jacksonville, North Carolina to be at O.B Lee's bedside when he was dying. O.B. was the third member of what several Texas and Mississippi council members referred to as the Florida mafia. We stuck together on most Gulf fishery issues and always together on Florida issues. We did our homework before debating our Texas friends on the Council.

When Captain Put died his family and friends were distraught, but their faith sustained them through the grieving process. Capt. Put was the kind of man you meet a few times in the trip through life and the kind of man you never forget.

B.J Putnam, O.B. Lee, Gene Raffield and I were close

friends from the first moment we met. We recognized and accepted each others warts and moved beyond them, forming strong relationships that lasted to the end.

All three of my friends have died, but I think of them often. I keep them in my prayers at Mass. I still play Hearts with them on my computer. The computer Hearts game lets you select the names of the other three players, so Gene is on my left, O.B. is across from me, and Captain Put is on my right. Many times the phone rings and friends ask Mindy, my wife, if I'm home. She's often said, "Yes, he's on his computer playing Hearts with his three buddies."

Most people who call at home at night know me so they are not too surprised with whatever I'm doing. Mindy has had to explain the Hearts game to the uninitiated, but my kids and friends know me and accept my spirituality and the fact I march to the beat of a different drum.

Some nights the trio gang up on me and stick me with the Queen of Spades three or four hands in a row. When that happens I tell them goodnight and close the game down for the evening. I don't think I'm weird because I'm enjoying fond memories of three good men. Once we were four - only one is standing.

I finished writing this chapter around 10:00 PM one evening, so I thought I'd play a quick game of Hearts before going to bed. I clicked the Heart icon on my desktop and up came the game with the first hand already dealt.

My hand contained zero spades and I started to smile. I selected three high clubs to pass to Gene who was on my left, but before sending them, I said out loud to my-self, "If Put passes me the singleton Queen of spades which becomes the only spade in my hand; something is going on beyond my comprehension."

I swear on all things holy that when I clicked the mouse to send my three clubs to Gene, I got two high hearts and the Queen of Spades from Put. I looked at that Queen and felt the big grin form as my eyes moistened. I said in a very quiet, melancholy voice, "Goodnight boys" as I closed the game of hearts.

CHAPTER 19

Ralph & Kitty Aylesworth Legacy

RALPH AYLESWORTH WAS FIVE-YEARS-OLD WHEN HIS WIDOWED MOTHER BROUGHT THE FAMILY TO ST. PETERSBURG FROM NEW YORK IN 1926. Ralph grew up quickly in a rough and tumble era. He was known for his integrlty, soft voice and ability to work without much rest, beginning with his first job. Bobby Aylesworth, Ralph and Kitty's son said, "I imagine they looked like the Beverly Hillbillies with all their worldly goods in and on top of their old sedan headed south down the highway."

The Aylesworth's launched their fishing career during hard times called the Hoover Days. The Great Depression was in full-swing. They struggled to pay their bills. It was necessary for Ralph to work at odd-jobs to make ends meet and then work more hours cleaning fish.

The Aylesworth's first business was located on Florida's Gulfport Pier. They packed and sold fish bait to their pier fishing customers and also bought fish from them including grouper, snapper, snook, mullet, pan-fish and live crabs. Like other fishing pier entrepreneurs of that era, the Aylesworth's facility was the size of a large bedroom and located half-way out on the pier.

There were no state or federal fishing licenses required so all species of fish of any size could be sold by the pier fishermen. The Aylesworths were delighted to buy them and sell the fresh fish in their retail market. Ralph and other fishing pioneers depended on the "Bucket Brigade" to supply fresh fish to their customers. The bucket brigade was composed mostly of winter tourists who fished for fun and sold their catch to pay living expenses. Lots of local characters also fished from the pier to make walking-around money for cigarettes and wine.

The bucket brigades were active for over fifty years until the Florida Marine Fisheries Commission was created in 1983. It was not long before the new commissioners prohibited recreational bridge fishermen from selling their fresh fish unless they possessed a commercial fishing license.

The only way to qualify for a commercial fishing license was to prove 50% of your income came from commercial fishing. Very few, if any, tourist could prove half their income came from commercial fishing. As a result they were stopped from making extra money and providing fresh fish to the market. The politically based ban on sales of legal size fish by pier fishermen hurt thousands of consumers who lost access to fresh fish.

The Aylesworth's Seafood Company operated in Gulfport until 1958 when they moved to their current location at 1295 28th Street South in St. Petersburg. They formed a trucking business the same year and delivered fish products throughout the United States. Sonny Aylesworth was a key to the success of the company.

Their fish business was always a family affair, the

same as most pioneer commercial fishing families. When a thousand pounds of mullet were placed on the cutting table in their processing plant, Kitty Aylesworth stood side by side with Ralph and brother-in-law Sonny Aylesworth - up to her ankles in mullet - during the roe-season. Her razor-sharp knife removed mullet roe without any nicks on the delicate and valuable by-product. Bobby Aylesworth said his mother could cut a 300-pound Warsaw grouper into serving-size fillets quicker than any fish-cutter in their plant or in the Tampa Bay area.

Kitty was outstanding not only in the cutting room but in handling the wide array of customers strolling through their retail markets swinging doors. Bobby Aylesworth said when you stand behind a fish counter in a white apron and white cap in the retail fish business you meet a lot of characters. Kitty could handle all of them from the nice to the not so nice.

During one twenty-year period in the 1970's and 1980s Pinellas County had four main-players in the seafood industry who were Ralph Aylesworth, Heber Bell, Leon Kenney and Charlie Rice. They were known in the fish trade as the Pinellas Four. Some of their competitors called them the Pineapple Four or worse. There are many other fish houses and fishermen with great narratives and experiences, but my book is about folks I knew and worked with in the Southeastern Fisheries Association.

The Pinellas Four sponsored a Hospitality Suite at each association convention. It was known as the Pinellas Gas

Pump, where the whiskey flowed freely. The tables in the hospitality room were stacked high with spiny lobster, shrimp and stone crab claws. It was a safe-haven for hard-working, hard-headed wheelers and dealers to stretch the truth and perform skullduggery against each other in a friendly atmosphere. It was a happy and memorable event where fish tales were exaggerated and retold, and tons and tons of Florida seafood was sold on a handshake or nod of the head. Written contracts between association members were not yet required.

Aylesworth Foundation for the Advancement of Marine Sciences

A Sea Grant statement on the front page of a University of Florida web site describes scholarship opportunities for students interested in science. It says, *"Ralph and Kitty Aylesworth, long-time members of the Florida fishing industry, established the Aylesworth Foundation for the Advancement of Marine Sciences in 1984. They created the foundation to make a long-term investment in the industry which has been so good to them and their family."*

The Aylesworth Foundation has improved the lives of at least eighty-five students at ten different universities in Florida. The scholarships are presented during Southeastern Fisheries Association's annual Awards Banquet. The award is prestigious. It is how one outstanding commercial fishing family says thank you to the industry that provided a livelihood for them all their lives. It is rewarding to see the smiles on young students faces as they receive financial help making their college education possible. **The Aylesworth Foundation is a proud legacy on behalf of the commercial fishing industry**.

CHAPTER 20

"On-Deck" For All Seasons

THERE IS ONLY ONE "ON-DECK." Some association members and some not even in the fish business have said one is enough. Others wish there was an "On-Deck" in every city. No matter where you fit into this spectrum Robert Wellington "On-Deck" Starr is unique. He is a staunch American patriot with the generational pedigree of a southern gentleman.

He served in WW II aboard the USS Marblehead, LC-12, an Omaha-type light cruiser built in 1924. Bob came aboard after the Marblehead had been hit in the Java Sea Battle. He told me that having pre-Pearl Harbor salts on the ship made life interesting for the young recruits. He had convoy duty escorting troops from Halifax, Nova Scotia to Belfast, Ireland. Part of the ship's assignment was to locate and sink German submarines carrying supplies from Argentina to the German ports.

The USS Marblehead also escorted supply ships and ships transporting Brazilian soldiers from Rio de Janeiro to Naples, Italy. Bob said most people do not know that Brazil sent troops to fight on the American's side during the war.

"One of the roughest trips I had was a 37-day voyage on a transport ship as a passenger", he recalled. "I thought it was a great adventure then because I was 17, but if I had to do it today it would kill me."

On this trip Bob was assigned to the 7th Fleet steaming toward the Pacific when President Harry Truman dropped the atomic bomb. His ship made a U-turn. It was quickly decommissioned at the Philadelphia Navy Yard in November of 1945. He was Honorably Discharged from the Navy in 1946.

With a strong, clear, operatic voice, Bob's baritone notes have filled hotel ballrooms for the past sixty years at the association's annual meetings. He is an octogenarian with a hard belly and a hard head to match. He has a smile that can light up a room and the wisdom to count all his fingers after dealing with a few of the sharks in the industry. He has seen every kind of seafood scam possible during his worldwide travels. He frequently reminisces about the era when trust was the glue holding the seafood brotherhood together.

Bob hails from Pensacola. He succumbed to the lure of the sea at an early age. After he was discharged in 1946, he was unable to find a job that paid more than $25 per week for 14 to 16 hours of hard work per day. Warriors then and warriors now don't receive as much help as they should when they are discharged.

With his extensive naval training he was hired as an able-bodied seaman on an ESSO tanker sailing the seven seas. When I asked him about his ports of call we determined he may have missed one bar on the outskirts of Zanzibar, but that's about it.

After three years with ESSO, the tanker returned to

dry-dock in Mobile. While on liberty Bob fell for a pretty young girl. As a result of his new romance and thinking everything over for at least twenty minutes, he and a buddy left the tanker business to make their fortunes as Alabama commercial blue-crabbers.

They bought a 30-foot wooden blue crab boat and named it *Mint Julip.* I wondered why he didn't name it *Manhattan* or *Old Granddad* or just plain *Highball,* but *Mint Julip* was politically correct in this bastion of southern gentility known as lower Alabama.

They navigated the red and green buoys obeying the inland rules of the road as they sailed the *Mint Julip* from Mobile to Bayou La Batre. After a few unsuccessful attempts looking for a friendly dock owner, they found a wholesale dealer with dock space who said he'd pay them ten cents per pound for their crabs. He told them the big crab migration was coming so they were satisfied to eke out a living until then.

When the big crab run started they caught so many their boat's freeboard was just above the water. The big, strong blue crabs scampered all over the boat biting anything they could get their claws on.

As often happens when a market is glutted, the dealer lowered the price the fourth day of heavy production to three cents a pound which was still pretty good money in those days for a single man working as a crabber.

A few days later the dealer allowed them to crab every third day. They didn't make gas money even though fuel was thirty-three cents a gallon. Their venture into the crab business to make a fortune collapsed. They tried to sell the *Mint Julip*. Nobody wanted it. With total frustration and a little anger the wannabee crabbers tied the *Mint Julip* to a broken down dock on the Dog River and hitchhiked back to Mobile searching for a better way to earn a living.

Things really went bad for Bob because the girl he met jilted him when he called to say he was back. She said, "You spent too much time crabbing and not enough time with me."

I'm not absolutely sure because I wasn't there, but I bet Bob was speechless and that is hard to believe by anyone who knows him.

He scrounged around the Mobile and Pensacola waterfronts looking for work at sea. He was worn out from being the "star of bar" in Pensacola juke joints. He says he got lucky and was hired as a crewman on a snapper boat. He learned a lot working for Victor Gonzales, owner of the famous Star Fish Company.

Bob quickly learned the secrets of the fishing trade. After many trips with Star Fish (an appropriate company for Bob Starr) he decided to fish for Pensacola's E.E. Saunders Fish Company. He worked hard during the thirty and forty day trips to Mexico's Alacon Reef. He figured quickly that the most important man on the ship was the old-man in charge of icing the fish. Everybody's share depended on the ice man doing his job well to maintain the highest quality of the red snapper.

On June 25, 1950, the Korean War started. Federal regulations required licensed American crews on all ships carrying cargo to Korea during the war. As an able body seaman with all requisite papers, Bob went back to work on the ESSO tankers. He sailed to every port in the Gulf of Mexico and the east coast of the nation, but never made a trip to Seoul. The trip he remembers the most was loading the ship with oil at Lake Maracaibo and delivering it to Helsinki. The length of his shore leave allowed a visit to Lapland and then back to Syria for more oil to deliver. He stayed with ESSO until the end of the war in July of 1953.

When he returned to Pensacola his father advised him not to keep living life the way he always did. "You need to get a regular job," his father told him more than once.

After working at regular jobs for a while, Bob took off the nice clothes, put on his dancing shoes and headed out to make his fortune in the seafood industry.

"One of the best things that ever happened to me was meeting Joe Patti," Bob said in a reflective tone of voice. "On a scale of 1 to 10, Joe Patti was a 10+. We were friends until the day he died. I still do business with Frank occasionally and think about the kind old skipper most every day."

Working with Joe Patti, Bob traveled to the Yucatan and met the American fishermen who were harvesting red snapper. Joe Patti and Sal Piazza of New Orleans helped Bob buy fresh red snapper and ship them to the US.

Bob always listened to Joe and Sal concerning the fishing business. He credits his at-sea-education as the reason he did well in the seafood industry. He made regular trips to Mexico until the Mexicans learned how to rig their own boats and gear and no longer had a need for American fishing expertise. His business in Mexico came to an end.

A.J. "Roby" Robida, one of Bob's longtime friends, was the first president of Southeastern Fisheries Association when it was founded in 1952. Roby had a highly successful fish business in Jacksonville and he trusted Bob very much. Roby needed surgery and was slated for ninety days of recuperation so he asked Bob to work at Florida Fish Distributors while he was recuperating. Bob agreed. He learned a great deal about the inner-workings of the fish business and found much of it very interesting, but on his ninety-first day in Jacksonville he left right after Roby walked through the door that afternoon.

While Bob worked in Jacksonville he was given an opportunity to establish a fish processing plant in Spanish Honduras. He bought a permit and licenses to harvest fishery products and export them to Miami for a period of eighteen months.

The first thing he did was lease the dreadnaught *Kermack,* a ninety-one foot WW II wooden minesweeper. He refurbished the boat and installed multiple freezers. He loaded it with every type of fishing gear he could buy and sailed off to Spanish Honduras in search of his fortune.

He had six men in his crew. They pulled lobster traps, dove for conch and harvested all available species of fish. He operated from a plant at Coxen Hole on Roatan Island.

He bought fish from other fishermen and fish houses to have enough seafood for a full load to ship to Miami.

He froze his seafood on the *Kermack* and wrapped it in sisal bags. They transferred the frozen seafood to a large freezer ship that stopped once a month on the way to Miami. Bob always asked the captain to call Richard Black at Superior Fish Company in Miami to come pick up the shipment. Sam Cooper, who owned Angelo's Seafood in Fort Lauderdale, purchased all the whole fish. A month after the delivery Bob flew to Miami to pick up his checks from Richard and Sam. "That probably wouldn't work in today's world, but was business as usual in those days," Bob recently said.

One time Bob had ten thousand pounds of conch on his boat when the freezer broke down. The boat sailed to La Sabre where an ice plant was located, but the ice plant was out of operation. Lucky for Bob, Tampa's Sam Tringali, who was a pioneer in Florida's shrimping industry, had a fleet of shrimp boats in La Sabre and gave Bob as much ice as he could and still have enough ice for his own boats. It wasn't enough, but Bob never forgot Sam Tringali's kindness and generosity.

While he waited for the cargo freezer ship to arrive, he and his crew took turns jumping into the hold in waist-deep water to stir the conch meat around trying to get some ice on it. The freezer ship arrived, but was full. Bob asked the captain to put the conch meat as close to the freezer as possible. That was all he could do.

He wrote Ralph Aylesworth and asked the St. Petersburg seafood dealer and trucker to pick up and pack the conch meat or throw it away. Several months later Bob stopped by Ralph Aylesworth's office to see what he did with the conch meat. Bob asked Ralph if he remembered the conch meat. Ralph said yes and he had a check for him. Bob almost fainted because he didn't think he would get anything for the conch meat.

"Did it kill anybody?" Bob asked.

"No, "Ralph said with a grin. " Customers keep asking me when am I going to get more of that funny looking conch meat that tasted so different." They both chuckled.

Those were the golden days when the seafood industry was fun. It was before the radical greenies established programs to destroy the commercial fishing culture.

There are so many stories about Bob Starr, but they'll have to wait for Part Two of this Trilogy. Suffice to say Diane, Bob's devoted wife, is doing all she can to keep "On Deck" up and at 'em.

Southeastern Fisheries Association hopes and prays Robert Wellington Starr continues delivering the same meaningful cheer he has given for the past forty-eight years.

With his fists balled up and his tattooed arms reaching for the ceiling his basso profundo voice proudly challenges everyone by proclaiming, "We gonna sing and we gonna dance, come on Southeastern we've got a chance!"

CHAPTER 21

Holy Mackerel

TOM HILL, PRESIDENT OF KEY LARGO FISHERIES INC., SENT ME A
NOTE ABOUT A CONVERSATION BETWEEN HIS FATHER AND A MULTI-
MILLIONAIRE LAND DEVELOPER WHO WAS SERVING AS CHAIRMAN OF
THE FLORIDA MARINE FISHERIES COMMISSION.

"George Barley and my dad were riding on a sightseeing boat with a group of dignitaries looking at the
John Pennekamp Sanctuary during the mid-1980s," Tom
wrote. "It was the time fishing boundaries in the Keys
were being hotly debated."

"Jack Hill," George Barley said, "You need to get a
glass bottom boat 'cause all you are going to be able to
do is look at the fish, not catch 'em."

Little did anyone in the Florida fishing industry realize
the beginning of hard times was upon them. The unwrit-
ten, long range plan of the anti-commercial fishing crowd
was to remove fish management from the legislature
which offered too many opportunities for the truth from
both sides of an issue to be heard before the final vote
was cast. The first step in their plan was to create the
Marine Fisheries Commission whose rules had to be approved by the Governor and Cabinet for at least a few
years. There would be no legislative committee oversight.

Southeastern Fisheries Association opposed having

fishing regulations excluded from overview by the legislature, but felt there might be a chance under the supervision of the elected Cabinet. Fair hearings and open decisions were made for awhile, but slowly and surely the newly elected Cabinet members wanted out from fish management because fish issues are always controversial. They did not like to face a meeting room full of angry people every time a fish issue came up.

A decade later the same special interests that created the Marine Fisheries Commission launched a program to ban commercial fishing nets in Florida waters. They sold the public a bill of goods promising them if they voted to ban fishing nets, "Florida fish would become so plentiful it would be like the early days of statehood." In truth, the recreational fishermen have been savaged almost as much as the commercial fishermen since the net ban.

I met Jack and Dottie Hill in August of 1964 when Malinda and our four children Mike, Cindy, Laurie and Mark, (Matthew was on the way) visited Key Largo. None of us had ever been to the Keys, except my mother Frances Jones, who lived in Key West as a child. Jack Hill was a spiny lobster fisherman and a natural born leader.

Our first gorgeous morning in Key Largo, Malinda and I drove to the dock where his boat, the *Minnehaha* was tied up waiting for us. We headed offshore with Jack and one crewman to pull crawfish traps while my mother entertained the kids at the historic Key Largo Lodge.

Jack took us trolling in the Gulf Stream after all traps

were pulled. We were in sight of land in very deep water. This was strange because Malinda and I grew up in St. Augustine where the Gulf Stream is 55 miles east of the beach.

Malinda kept glancing at a massive cargo ship, bigger than any building in Tallahassee, swiftly bearing down on us from the north. She nervously asked Jack, "Are we in the way?"

"Nope," he responded. "No problem".

When the cargo ship passed by, and just before Malinda had apoplexy, Jack gunned the engine, cut sharply to the starboard and trolled within what seemed to me to be 100 feet of the giant ship's stern. Something big hit the fishing line, immediately. Mindy was very nervous. I wasn't all that calm myself, but I trusted Jack Hill. He said big fish sometimes follow ships that dump garbage. Jack snatched the well-worn bamboo fishing pole out of the rod holder, handed it to Malinda and told her to reel in the prize.

She was winding real hard, doing a grand job bringing a large bonito to the stern of the *Minnehaha.* All of a sudden we saw a massive swirl and the line went slack. She kept reeling, but the only catch was the bloody head of the bonito, still moving its gills. It didn't know it was dead yet. A powerful set of big jaws ate everything else quicker than you can snap your fingers. Mindy looked at the bloody head, looked at me and I knew she was ready to get back to shore. This fishing trip in August 1964 was the only time I ever fished with Jack Hill.

Jack and Dottie Hill, along with sons Tom and Rick, were struggling fish house operators in the early 1970s, the same as other fishermen making the transition from fisherman to fish house owner. The Jack Hill Bait and Seafood Company poured every dime it made back into the business. The family built a cooler, a freezer, tables and anything they could because they had no money to buy equipment. The money was so tight during the Christmas of 1973 that Tom came home from Oral Roberts University in Tulsa, Oklahoma to help the family by working at the fish house. Dottie was the manager of the Tom Thumb convenience store, bringing home enough money to sustain the family's basic needs, but the hours were long and when she got home there were still lots of chores waiting.

Finances got extremely tight. Jack told the family there was only enough money for one more bank payment on their building. The Hill family was in the darkest, most menacing part of their financial storm. They said a prayer of thanks and placed their needs and hopes in their Higher Power.

Prior to schools of Spanish mackerel making their migratory run to the south, a small run happened near Key Largo. Fisherman Lloyd Winsted and his mate, John Gooding, caught some mackerel then helped Jack design and build a washer/chiller device to handle mackerel in an efficient manner.

During the first week of January 1974, a massive run

of Spanish mackerel showed up about a quarter of a mile from Jack Hill Bait and Seafood. That's when things began popping at the fish house. Gene Raffield, one of the greatest innovators ever in the Florida fishing industry, sent his brothers Harold, Ronnie and Danny to Key Largo to help handle the Spanish mackerel bonanza.

The Raffield's loaded their 18-wheelers with fully iced Spanish mackerel three or four days a week for the next six to eight weeks. Some days the Hill's worked around the clock. On good days they slept four hours before washing their face, putting on clean clothes and heading back to the fish house full of mackerel. They hired folks from their church who worked from sunrise to sunset. The high school students on the crew worked when they got out of school, but all went home at dark. The night shift belonged to the Hill family.

The unloading process was primitive compared to today, but got much better when Jack began putting four baskets on a pallet and lowering it into the boat for the fisherman to fill. Each basket held 102 pounds so, if the fisherman had about 8,000 pounds in the fish boxes, it would take twenty operations with the hoist to unload the boat. Most times the Spanish mackerel gillnet boats were five deep tied to the dock and fifteen or twenty boats with their engines idling waiting for their turn in the queue.

Over the eight-week period, Jack Hill Bait and Seafood handled almost a million pounds of Spanish mackerel, allowing the Hill family to finish their building and in 1976 it became Key Largo Fisheries, a top of the line fisheries operation.

A CULTURE WORTH SAVING

Tom Hill told me something I quote directly.

"One cold night I was working by myself unloading the boats, washing the fish and putting the fish in the cooler. At about 2:00 AM I remember praying, "Lord, I sure could use some help." It was not long before two guys walked up and said they were looking for work. Looking for work at 2:00 AM in the morning? I told one guy to crush ice and the other helped me pack and stack fish in the cooler. At about 8:00 AM my crew came in and the two guys came to me and said okay, we are done here, please pay me. I paid them for about seven hours worth of work and they were gone. I later thought about what the Bible says about entertaining angels. To this day I think God sent me two angels to help me during the night."

Spanish mackerel had never made a run like the one it made in 1974 according to fishermen who lived in Key Largo for decades. Spanish mackerel have never made another run in Key Largo since then. I agree with Tom Hill about angels and I think this was truly a sign.

Were the fish that appeared once in a lifetime off Key Largo close to Jack Hill Bait and Seafood Company truly Holy Mackerel?

Yes, I think they were and that says it all.

CHAPTER 22

Fisherman meets Congressman

CLYDE KITCHEL WAS AN EAST COAST SEAFOOD DEALER WHO SETTLED IN EAU GALLIE, FLORIDA IN 1950. He was a past president of Southeastern Fisheries Association, a river and inshore gillnet fisherman, crabber and operated his small retail market in back of his house in Eau Gallie. He was a well read street-fighter and hardcore fisherman with total confidence in himself and his abilities.

The first time I met Clyde he was scaling and cutting mullet on a wooden table outside his retail market. I was wearing new khaki trousers and an open collared shirt. He asked if I knew how to clean fish. I said yes. I got his message and moved to the cutting table. For two hours I scaled and gutted mullet. No matter how hard I tried to prevent it from happening my clothes got wet and dirty. But the worse thing was my only pair of dress shoes smelled like fish juice. I had other clothes, but not any other shoes for the week long trip to South Florida.

Clyde and his wife Avice were taking me out to dinner. I was spending the night with them to save travel funds.

He showed me my bedroom and the bathroom to wash mullet scales out of my hair and off my skin. I wrapped my fish-cleaning clothes and put them in a plastic bag. I tied the knot real tight. I put everything I could find with a sweet smell on my shoes. I used everything from shaving cream to Old Spice deodorant, but no matter what I did my shoes retained the distinct aroma of fish juice.

Clyde was impressed that I not only knew how to clean mullet, but that I helped clean them for his retail market. We bonded that evening and stayed in touch the rest of the time he belonged to the association.

The down side of this encounter was when I got dressed the next morning and put on my fish-juice shoes. Both of Clyde's cats sniffed and scratched at my shoes until I got into the car and headed to Fort Lauderdale and Miami. I prayed the other association members I would meet didn't have cats to follow me around thinking I was a case of Meow-Mix.

When Clyde was part of a delegation of association members flying to Washington, D.C. to host a seafood banquet for the Florida Congressional Delegation he made his real mark. Clyde was famous for his crab salad and after the Florida seafood feast we were in the kitchen cleaning up pots and pans when Congressman Don Fuqua, (D) from Altha, Florida walked over to tell us how much he enjoyed the meal, especially the crab salad. I introduced him to Clyde Kitchel.

The Congressman said, "Glad to meet you Mr. Kitchen."

Clyde stopped washing a big pot and deftly pulled his pipe out of his mouth. I saw his feet move into a defensive position and wondered what was next. I sure hoped he didn't throw a punch at a voting member of Congress.

Clyde put a knurled, weather-cracked index finger on the Congressman's chest and said in a low, stern voice, "My name in Kitchel."

Using his finger as a pointer and sinking it into the Congressman's chest with each letter, he spelled out his name, an act which I can still see him doing quite vividly,

"K I T C H E L, Kitchel. You got it?"

The Congressman said. "Yes."

Congressman Fuqua never forgot Clyde Kitchel's name and he and I often laughed about his special spelling lesson.

CHAPTER 23

Riding the River with Rayburn

IF I AM EVER ASKED TO DESCRIBE RALPH R. RAYBURN OF TEXAS IN ONE SENTENCE I WOULD SAY, *"RALPH WAS A MAN TO RIDE THE RIVER WITH."* This is the same high compliment my friend Walter Wilder used at his best friend's funeral. The name of Walter's best friend was Gene Raffield from Port St. Joe.

Over thirty-three years ago, Ralph Rayburn was selected executive director of the Texas Shrimp Association. I knew all his predecessors from the first director Jim Barr, then Oscar Longnecker, Bob Mauermann, Lucy Gibbs and finally Ralph Rayburn. He was the new kid on the block when we met in 1978.

As director of the Texas Shrimp Association Ralph automatically became a Trustee of the Gulf and South Atlantic Fisheries Development Foundation. He was elected President of the Foundation in 1987 and remained a Trustee until he left the Texas Shrimp Association in 1990.

Ralph was instrumental in restructuring the Foundation's financial procedures after the audit from hell conducted by the Office of Inspector General. I think that audit was politically inspired, but it had the effect of putting the Foundation on a strong, transparent financial footing which is still in place.

A CULTURE WORTH SAVING

I had served as Executive Director of Southeastern Fisheries Association for fourteen years by the time I met Ralph. I already had a plethora of scars all over my back and buttocks by then. But even with fourteen years in the trenches of fish warfare I wasn't prepared for what was about to occur. I had no idea that in a few short years Ralph and I would be up that well known creek without a paddle. However, when we found ourselves there we knew the direction we were trying to go was the right direction even without a paddle.

Prior to the passage of the Magnuson Act which extended the sovereignty of the United States over fisheries out to 200 miles from shore, our Gulf of Mexico shrimp fleet was fishing far and wide and the fishery was quite robust. That is usually the case when a marine species has a one year life span.

Shrimp boats were being churned out on an assembly line basis during the previous decade. Some major shrimp companies were seeing signs of change in the catch per unit of effort within their fleet.

This was all about to change forever for the domestic shrimp industry. The Magnuson Act extended U.S. rights over Gulf waters out to 200 miles, but we had very few foreign vessels fishing in the Gulf of Mexico. Conversely, we had over 2,000 U.S. vessels shrimping and fishing off Mexico and Central and South America. Our distant water fleet was in harm's way as all coastal nations of the world followed the US lead and extended their sovereignty out to 200 miles from shore.

After the Magnuson fish management legislation was enacted and implemented Ralph and I participated in the Joint US-Mexican Shrimp Talks in Mexico City. We tried to persuade Mexico to permit our continued shrimping on historical shrimping grounds we shrimped prior to the Magnuson Act. We requested that, at the very least, the government faze us out over an extended period of time.

We did not succeed because the Mexican Cooperativa's demanded that all US fishermen be removed from their waters. It was a very good experience for me to serve as an advisor to the U.S. State Department and to have the opportunity to see how foreign relations should work, even though they did not in this instance.

Ralph and I succeeded, through the Gulf and South Atlantic Fisheries Development Foundation trustees, to fund projects on quality control, marketing, and economic projects that might assist fishermen returning to the Gulf from shrimp, reef fish and spiny lobster distant water fishing fleets.

We stayed busy laboring in the vineyards of commercial fishing issues at the state, national and international level. Although there was a dedicated alliance of sport fishing militants and a few radical outdoor writers spewing hatred for all things commercial, their efforts paled when compared to what was about to happen concerning sea turtles.

When I became Executive Director of Southeastern Fisheries Association in 1964 there was a viable, commercial turtle fishery. Sea turtles were legally harvested, landed and butchered. The turtle kraal was a large open air tourist attraction and fish house in downtown Key West. The roof was held up by massive pilings connected to worn wooden walkways between the turtle pens. The live turtles were harvested locally and from throughout the Caribbean. They were separated in pens based on species and size. The turtles were butchered and then canned for soup or served as fresh turtle steaks in local restaurants and in high-end restaurants throughout the U.S. Their shells were carved into jewelry and all kind of tourist doodads.

This turtle fishery was healthy according to the few fishermen in the business as well as the fishery managers. They never saw any decline in the stocks throughout their career according to personal communications with Edwin Felton and other "Conchs" who lived in Key West. Turtles, to them, were food just like any other marine resource.

Marine turtles were used for food and trade for the past 100 years and were a major part of the Native Americans diet for centuries. They are not used for food any more in the United States.

In 1973, the Endangered Species Act was passed by Congress and signed into law by President Richard Nixon. The first US fishery to feel the impact of the Endangered Species Act was the tuna fishing industry. The highly efficient, mostly California tuna purse seiners surrounded large schools of tuna that the porpoises were feeding on in the ocean. When the tuna were bailed from the net to the fishing hold dead porpoises were often bailed on board as well. The photos of porpoises hanging in large tuna nets made worldwide press. These photos were the genesis for the sustained hatred of commercial fishing that is still alive and building in many parts of the United States.

After investigating the tuna operation and gathering evidence of what happens on board the purse seine vessels, environmental leaders were able to use the Endangered Species Act to prohibit the harvest of purse seine caught tuna by American tuna fishermen on the high seas anywhere in the world.

The environmentalists had already used the Act to stop a huge hydro-electric project from being built by the Tennessee Valley Authority because of the Snail Darter so stopping tuna fishing was not all that difficult for them to accomplish.

The tuna industry, at that time, was one of the most powerful fishery trade associations in the country. Their Washington lobbyists were legends. Charlie "the tuna" Carey and Augie Felando were zealots for their constituency. They verbally dominated any meeting for fishing sectors. During one State Department Fishery Advisory Committee meetings, when Ambassador Don Mc Kernan was chairman I asked for equal time to discuss Gulf of Mexico shrimp and spiny lobster problems and got it.

Shrimp and spiny lobster issues were usually at the bottom of the agenda with tuna, salmon and halibut getting most of the air time. There could be an entire book written on these two tuna legends and other fishery groups of the time but my short story is about someone

I have ridden the river with, not the tuna boys.

It wasn't long after their success in bringing the tuna industry under control that Washington-based environmental leaders set their sights on saving the sea turtle. The United States shrimp industry has never been the same. It never will be.

The professionals running the fishery trade associations knew sea turtles were about to become the poster child for the environmental movement and that millions upon millions of federal dollars would be spent to save marine turtles. We knew the shrimp industry was about to be heavily regulated under the Endangered Species Act. Ralph and I knew turtle excluder devices (TEDS) would be mandated. It was only a matter of time. We needed to find a way to comply with the law and a way to talk to the environmentalists.

Sea turtles are beautiful animals that lay eggs infrequently on certain beaches and can live one hundred and fifty years as opposed to a Southern shrimp that lives one year. The sea turtle is a critter that cannot stand worldwide exploitation and survive. It is possible that a particular sea turtle species can become extinct, but the chance is remote, regardless of the rhetoric.

The sea turtle is a mysterious, unassuming, un-aggressive, peaceful animal that some folks look upon as magical or spiritual. As an example, at a fisheries meeting in New Orleans, an environmental speaker was presenting a very informative report on the Kemp's Ridley turtle and its comeback. The Kemp's Ridley population is recovering since conservation efforts were implemented in

Mexico in the specific area where thousands of Kemp's Ridley females nest each year.

The speaker said watching a turtle make its way to the beach, dig a nest and then lay its eggs was like a religious experience. I certainly felt the religious experience at the birth of my children and grandchildren, but not a turtle. Herein lays the greatest challenge to fish managers because children are often being taught certain critters of the sea are more important than humans.

Professional trade association executives knew things were going to change and the best approach would be to help ease the changes for their members.

The National Marine Fisheries Service offered a great deal of input through Jack Brawner who became Regional Director for the National Marine Fisheries Service later in his career. He advised Ralph and me and other leaders of the shrimping industry about the benefits of meeting with the environmental leaders and establishing a relationship. Brawner suggested the two groups work together to solve the turtle mortality problem associated with trawling without closing the shrimp industry down the way the tuna industry had been closed.

A series of meetings was held between leaders of the shrimp associations and independent shrimpers and then with the environmentalists. After numerous meetings and more heated rhetoric than I care to recall, we held a final meeting in Washington D.C. with the environmental leaders.

Ralph Rayburn from Texas, Bob Jones from Florida and T. John Mijalivic from Louisiana were invited. Prior to the meeting the three groups received a draft of an agreement setting the stage for a cooperative effort establishing the use of turtle excluder devices. From my recollection, Rayburn and I signed the agreement on behalf of our members, but Mijalivic did not sign. When he returned to Louisiana all hell broke loose.

Ralph came under severe criticism from many shrimpers in Texas who demanded he take his name off the letter. I took a lot of heat but my Board of Directors stuck by the decision for me to sign the agreement with the environmentalists on behalf of the association. They understood the ramifications of the agreement and supported my name staying on the letter. I had made a commitment on behalf of the association and was not about to renege on it.

It didn't take long for the demagogues to launch a campaign against turtle excluder devices. Mijalivic formed a shrimp association and paraded around the whole Gulf of Mexico coast promising shrimpers they would never have to pull turtle excluder devices and telling them that they needed to eat more turtle soup. I recall a news article showing him standing in the bed of a pickup truck in Key West holding a sign with a turtle recipe on it. He made the state newspapers and many environmental publications. The only thing he accomplished in Florida was make all shrimpers look like Neanderthals.

Mike Weber, an environmental leader, describes one scene very well in his book, *From Abundance to Scarcity, A History of U.S. Marine Fisheries Policy,* published by the Island Press www.islandpress.org. *"The whistles* *and cheers of 5,000 shrimp fishermen and their families filled the convention center in Thibodaux, Louisiana as Governor Edwin Edwards approached the microphone on a spotlight stage. Applause gave way to silence. <u>The governor began: If it comes between shrimpers and sea turtles......bye bye turtles.</u>" The bleachers shook beneath thousands of feet beating in agreement. The governor paused, and then dared the federal government to require shrimp fishermen to install turtle excluder devices (TEDS) in their nets. "The same federal government that has tried to put me in jail is trying to make you pull these turtle excluder devices." Hoots and guffaws swept through the convention hall. "*

Governor Edwards was at his zenith on that day in the late 1980s. But on January 9th, 2001, the 73 year old former Governor was sentenced to 10 years in federal prison on racketeering charges. Former San Francisco 49ers owner Edward de Bartolo Jr. said Edwards extorted $100,000 from him to obtain a gambling license. In 2005, Edwards was moved to a federal correctional institution in Oakdale, Louisiana and is scheduled to be released in 2011.

All the hard work we accomplished on behalf of the shrimp industry for decades meant nothing. It was now all about TEDS and Ralph and me "selling the industry out to the environmentalists." We were vilified beyond belief. The hatred toward me and Southeastern Fisheries Association was hard to take. The scorched earth policy by the demagogues was unstoppable and had to play out to the end. I told Ralph to lick his wounds and bide his time until the tide turns. It always does.

Every time Ralph and I saw some stupid statement like "eat more turtles" or "you have to kill me before I pull Teds," we shuddered because all this was doing was painting an image of the domestic shrimpers that would stay in the minds of the environmentalists all their lives. It has been over 30 years since this self-destructing drama happened and the Gulf shrimp industry is still suffering for its hard line against turtle conservation. They ignored that brief moment in time when they could have worked with other interest groups on a legitimate turtle issue.

From my perspective, the anti-Ted leaders did more damage to the image of the commercial fishing industry in general and the Gulf shrimper in particular than anything else has ever done. The quotes and actions of the hard core shrimp spokesmen gave the environmentalists what they needed to get their way not only with the federal agencies, but Congress and the world media as well. The mean-spirited, hateful rhetoric toward the turtle conservationists and regulators still makes survival difficult for the shrimpers still in the fishery.

The sad part of this for me is there are still sons of two former association presidents who dislike me so much for trying to solve the turtle problem they dropped out of the association responsible for saving the Florida pink shrimp resource for them and all who follow. I have not seen them or spoken to them since the day I signed the agreement with the environmentalists. The ill-feelings towards me put there by the demagogues is unforgivable. I miss seeing these two fine young men.

Ralph suffered more than I did for doing the right thing. The Texas Shrimp Association is about nothing but shrimp. Southeastern Fisheries Association represents all fisheries and segments, as well as shrimp.

It was during this tumultuous turtle ordeal that Ralph Rayburn and I rode the river. We had a special bond that only happens when you know you did the right thing for the right reason and you don't have to look back or apologize to anyone for your actions.

Ralph's commitment to the Texas shrimp industry, his courage, his patriotism, his honesty and integrity truly made him, *"**A man to ride the river with**."*

CHAPTER 24

Florida legislators helped fishermen

I MET REPRESENTATIVE RALPH TURLINGTON AT A GAINESVILLE HOSPI-
TAL IN 1966 WHEN HE VISITED MY FATHER-IN-LAW, REPRESENTATIVE
F. CHARLES USINA. Usina was suffering with terminal cancer
that took his life on May 31, 1966. He was recognized
by the Florida Legislature less than a month later with the
following comments.

*"In a June 28, 1966 Resolution of the Democratic
Caucus of Nominees for the Florida State Senate, presented to Representative Usina's widow, it was noted
that he was memorialized as the "conscience of the
House of Representatives" and "a man of unquestioned
integrity and devotion to his family and church, a good
companion to his friends and fellow members of the
Legislature... and an inspiration to those who follow in
his footsteps."*

The Usina family was in the room when Turlington
came in and pulled a chair close to the bed so he and
Usina could talk. They chatted for a few minutes and
laughed about some of their shared experiences in the
Florida House of Representatives. I remember when
Turlington got ready to leave Usina shook his hand and
said,

"Take care of Bobby."

Turlington nodded his head and left.

That was another moment in my life when I did not appreciate the significance of four words. I was so naïve that when we had a fish issue during the 1967 legislative session and I would ask for an appointment with the Speaker, I always got it. I thought everybody got the same treatment and did not realize that Usina's hand was still helping me, Malinda and his grandchildren. I'm not sure how many years it took me to have my epiphany, but I remember vividly sitting back in my chair at the office and being very quiet and very calm and very moved when I realized I was being helped by so many others because of four words that Usina said,.

"Take care of Bobby."

Ralph Turlington did "take care of Bobby" during his legislative career and his years on the Florida Cabinet when serving as Commissioner of Education.

Representative A.H. "Gus" Craig won Usina's seat which he had held for eleven terms from 1943 to 1966. Craig had served in the legislature with Usina, but didn't run against him when reapportionment reduced their legislative district seats from two to one. When Craig did return to the legislature, he had seniority and became Chairman of the Natural Resources Committee. I knew the Florida fishing industry's views would be considered and we would always get a fair hearing from Craig.

Senator Elmer O. Friday was proud to be a sixth generation Floridian. He absolutely loved everything about Florida's all-embracing history. He was born in Bartow, but lived most of his life in Lee and Collier counties.

FLORIDA LEGISLATORS HELPED FISHERMEN

He was a consummate outdoorsman from the moment he learned to walk. He served America during World War II and was among those who put it all on the line so the rest of us could enjoy freedom. He was a prominent University of Florida law school grad and a devout Gator fan for all things athletic, especially football.

Elmer served in the Florida Senate from 1962 through 1970. I met him in 1965 during my first year of lobbying. We were friends following our first conversation.

He represented one of the most robust commercial fishing areas in Florida. Lee and Collier counties produced millions of pounds of mullet and traded with Cuba and Native Americans long before Florida became a state.

He was a long time friend of shrimp industry leaders John Ferguson, Paul Herring, Larry Shafer, Bob Villers, Carl Erickson, Jack Costello, Ray Simmons, Joe and Angelo Militello, Marion Hagan, Charles, Hilbert and Donald Kiesel, Ralph Andrews, Mike Basseta, Jack d' Antignac and Dominic Tringali.

Elmer's district was blessed with every type of commercial fishery except oysters. Crab processor Ed Hendrickson and fish house owners, A.P. Bell, Jesse Padilla, Walter Gault, Bob Combs and Hewitt McGill were in his camp as well as commercial fisherman Floyd "Tootsie" Barnes who was a leader in the Organized Fishermen of Florida. Elmer respected Wayne Mead and Gene Mc Roberts even though they helped Leon Kenny stall the passage of the Tortugas shrimp bill for several years.

Elmer and Representative Ted Randell of Fort Myers

were the legislators most responsible for the establishment of the Tortugas Shrimp Nursery Area. Ninety percent of their constituents supported a no shrimp trawling area to perpetually protect the Florida pink shrimp resource.

It took several legislative sessions to pass the Tortugas nursery bill in the Florida Senate because there was a young, powerful, energetic senator from Pinellas County by the name of C.W. "Bill" Young. He was the minority leader from 1966 until 1970. Senatorial courtesy allowed him to kill the Tortugas shrimp no-trawling bill each session. He opposed our bill because his friend, Leon Kenney, did not want a no-trawling zone. Kenney's company would lose money if juvenile shrimp were protected from harvest.

Shrimp unloading facilities were paid according to the number of boxes of shrimp crossing their dock, not by the size of the shrimp inside the box. Juvenile shrimp filled more boxes than larger shrimp. This was the financial motivation to catch and unload as many boxes of shrimp as possible regardless of their size. A 100-count box of head-on shrimp made the shrimp dock the same amount of money as a box of 47-count heads-off shrimp and a boat could always bring in more boxes of what was called "hair and eyeballs" because baby shrimp were so plentiful.

Southeastern Fisheries Association got the bill passed in the House every session, but could not get it through the Senate and to the Governor's desk to sign into law. It was a real dog fight for five long years. There was a lot of money at stake. Some firms wanted to catch all the small shrimp before they could spawn instead of protecting the resource for future generations.

I remember the legislative session when I was confidentially told that Senator Young would not oppose the bill. Senator Friday immediately placed it on Special Orders in line for a full senate debate and final vote. Young's change of heart occurred because Leon Kenney rejoined Southeastern Fisheries Association and agreed to support majority rule.

As such, Kenney asked Senator Young not to defeat the bill. Senator Young removed his hold on the bill, but left the chamber when the vote was taken. He did not want to vote for it after killing it for so many years. We all understood.

I stood at my lucky spot outside the Senate chambers in the Old Capitol and held my breath during the final debate on the bill. Although Senator Young withdrew his opposition not all Senators did and some wanted to debate the issue one last time. I did not want to sit the gallery and listen to the discussion. After what seemed like an hour, the huge Senate Chamber doors flew open and Elmer walked quickly to the spot where I was leaning against the marble wall.

He had his well known full-grin on his face that said so much about his character and kindness. I knew he had passed the bill after years of hard work. He was a key in the battle creating a sustainable Florida pink shrimp industry.

I have respected Senator Young since I met him in 1965 and appreciate his continuing efforts on behalf of fisheries by his support of the Fish and Wildlife Research Institute in St. Petersburg. He left the Florida Senate in 1970 and won a seat in Congress which he still holds.

Panama City's Senator Dempsey J. Barron was one of the most remarkable and most powerful legislators I had the privilege to work with on behalf of Florida commercial fishing and rural school districts. We met in 1965 when I flew with Randolph Hodges to Panama City to interview Harmon Shields as Director of the new Bureau of Seafood Marketing. Harmon was a life-long friend of Barron and a friend of mine until the day he died.

I had no idea how powerful Hodges and Barron were in Florida politics. I was a thirty-one year old ex-bricklayer and a former U.S. Marine who was trying to absorb everything I could about the fishing industry and those who controlled its destiny.

I did not learn about Barron's heroic war service or his Navy ship being sunk in World War II until I read an obituary story by Lucy Morgan in the *St. Petersburg Times* in 2001. It was years before I learned Harmon Shields was a D-Day + 6 World War II army veteran. The WW II veterans never said much about what they did and I never pushed any of my friends for details.

Everything Barron did for the fishing industry was out of respect and friendship because we had no money to contribute for his election campaigns. We had shoe leather and word of mouth among the brotherhood.

Barron served in the House of Representatives from

1956 to 1960 and the Senate from 1960 to 1988. I considered him a mentor for twenty years.

He always listened to our side of a fishery issue and, more times than not, he supported what the fishing industry needed for survival.

CHAPTER 25
The Marine Fisheries Commission

THE MOST SIGNIFICANT FISHERY CHANGE ADVERSELY AFFECTING THE FLORIDA SEAFOOD INDUSTRY IN ITS HISTORY WAS THE CREATION OF THE MARINE FISHERIES COMMISSION BY THE 1983 FLORIDA LEGISLATURE. The concept and proposed language evolved from a two-year study on how Florida fisheries should be managed. The consensus, according to the final report, was a Marine Fisheries Commission should be created by law with the makeup of membership composed of two commercial fishermen, two recreational fisherman, two scientists and one environmentalist.

Fishing industry leaders felt anti-commercial fishing groups would remove all commercial fishing interests as soon as possible. We were promised, repeatedly, by the proponents that would not happen. But it did. Those who told us the composition of commission members would remain in place either lied or were naïve.

The bill creating the Marine Fisheries Commission was filed in the 1983 Florida Legislature. The fishing industry fought numerous amendments to remove the commission from any overview of oversight by elected officials. The proposed bill already removed one hundred sixty members of the Florida legislative. Now anti-fishing militants wanted to remove the six members of the

Florida Cabinet from oversight.

They only wanted a governor involved. That meant they needed to lobby and send campaign funds to one person. The two amendments we had to stop were the ones removing oversight of the cabinet and removing membership criteria for appointment to the commission.

Senator Dempsey Barron opposed the bill. He did not like appointed commissions. He said they tended to become a group of super egos who often felt they were above the law. The association did not like the bill either. The association's philosophy is elected officials must always have the final vote when decisions affecting a persons livelihood is made.

Senator Tom McPherson of Fort Lauderdale, Don Duden, in the top echelon of the Department of Natural Resources and George Barley, a land developer, pushed the bill hard. It was known as the McPherson Bill.

It was on the last day of the 1983 session, or next to the last day, when McPherson and Duden realized they couldn't get the bill on Special Orders and to the floor for a vote unless Barron released his hold on it.

Barron called me to his office. He asked me to check with the fishing industry to see if they could live with the latest version of the bill. He said unless I signed off on the bill he would not place it on Special Orders and the Marine Fisheries Commission bill would die this session.

I called Association president Leo Cooper and directors, Jack Hill, Joe Versaggi, B.J. Putnam, Bob Bell, Al Boromei, Sam Cooper, Gene Raffield, Clyde Richbourg, Bob Starr, Tony Lombardi, Jules de Nazarie and Richard

Griffin as well as many others throughout the state and informed them what Senator Barron told me and wanted to know what the fishing industry wanted him to do.

Every member told me to use my own judgment to let the bill pass or die. They all knew sooner or later this bill, or one that might be worse, would pass the Florida legislature.

I avoided talking to McPherson and Duden all morning because I was struggling hard to do the right thing for the right reason. When I saw them in the west senate gallery, I eased out of my seat in the east gallery and rode the elevator to the 10th floor cafeteria for a hot cup of coffee.

They caught up with me and said they really needed the bill and Senator Barron told them I had to sign off on it to get it on Special Orders. As much as I hated to do it I agreed. Then we walked to the Senate gallery. I got Senator Barron's attention while he was at his desk on the Senate floor. Mc Pherson and Duden were standing by me looking straight at him. I nodded my head to affirm that the industry agreed the bill should be passed. I gave my word to Mc Pherson and Duden that I would not do anything else to kill their legislation. I kept my word.

Later that day, Barron left the chamber as senators often do when they let a bill pass they do not like. Senator McPherson immediately made a motion to bring the Marine Fisheries Commission bill up for a vote. It passed easily. We all knew it would pass if it got to the floor for a vote. The day the marine fisheries commission bill became law was the day the Florida seafood industry became endangered and the management of Florida's marine resources was removed from legislative oversight forever.

Not long afterwards a list of nominees was submitted to Governor Bob Graham. The fishing industry recommended Tim Daniels from Marathon, Ed Felton from Key West, Blue Fulford from Cortez, Roger Newton from Apalachicola, Gene Raffield from Port St. Joe and Walter Spence from Niceville.

He appointed two recreational fishermen, two commercial fishermen, two scientists and one environmentalist. That was the only time the appointments were made according to the intent of the law.

I knew we were going to be in for a tough fight when one of Governor Graham's executive staff members called Gene Raffield. He said the Governor wanted George Barley to be elected chairman and hoped he would vote for Mr. Barley. High-level politics didn't take long to surface. Whether or not Governor Graham actually asked his aide to call Gene Raffield may never be known.

CHAPTER 26

Others who recognized the fishing culture

THERE HAVE BEEN MANY ELECTED OFFICIALS WHO HAVE HELPED THE FISHING INDUSTRY SURVIVE SINCE SOUTHEASTERN FISHERIES ASSOCIATION WAS FORMED SIX DECADES AGO. There are too many to list in these few chapters, but there were hundreds of good men and women who felt sympathy for the men and women of the sea.

Lawton Chiles was a stalwart supporter of commercial fishermen when he was in the Florida House, the Florida Senate, the U.S. Senate and a two-term governor. On several occasions, as governor, he asked the Marine Fisheries Commission to cut the commercial fishermen some slack, but they never did.

Every governor from Leroy Collins to Lawton Chiles had a warm spot in their hearts for commercial fishermen and Florida's seafood industry. I had the honor to meet Governor Collins in St. Augustine in 1960 when he came for a visit. He was an awesome governor, one of the greatest who ever served.

Governor Bob Graham was a friend of the commercial fishermen and performed one of his famous work days packing mullet at a processing facility in Niceville. I got to know him when he was a freshman state senator and filed a bill making permit a game fish.

I asked Senator Barron and several other senators to oppose the bill because we had a few fishermen in south Florida catching permit as part of their livelihood. The fishery was in good shape with the annual size of fish at harvest remaining steady because of mesh size regulations that allowed undersize fish to escape easily by swimming through the net.

I got a call from a wholesale dealer in Miami telling me that Jesse Webb and Al Pfleuger Jr., world-class fishermen from Miami, wanted the permit bill to pass real badly and would I talk to them. I said sure. We might have met in Graham's office or in the cafeteria. To make a long story short, the fish they were talking about was a specific species of permit, *trachinotus falcatus* which is a large, beautiful fish we did not want to catch. I told them to limit the bill to that species and we would not oppose it.

Senator Graham inserted the Latin name into his bill and it passed without a dissenting vote as I recall. I would love to ask the Senator to search one of his notebooks to see if he can find anything about *trachinotus falcatus.*

Governor Claude Kirk helped ban the use of purse seines to harvest food fish in state waters. He supported our marketing program and the industry worked with him on several events promoting the state by paying tribute to the baseball teams using Florida for their winter headquarters. Bunny Mick was his dollar a year sports liaison person who was a pleasure to work with on anything.

OTHERS WHO RECOGNIZED THE FISHING CULTURE

Governor Reuben Askew was a champion for the fishing culture when he was a state senator. He had a longstanding friendship with Clyde and Loretta Richbourg who owned American Seafood in his home town of Pensacola.

Governor Jeb Bush, a person I admired for many other reasons, supported the commercial fishing net ban in 1995 which we believe cost him the election against Chiles. The margin of victory over Bush was less than 70,000 votes statewide. The Florida Panhandle voted overwhelmingly for Chiles who opposed the net ban and said so in radio ads throughout Northwest Florida during the final month of the election.

Governor Charlie Crist, who followed Bush as governor, was also a net ban proponent and only after the oil spill was he truly helpful to the commercial fishing industry.

Governor Scott seems inclined to help working fishermen. His office has been open to input for recovery of the fishing industry after the BP oil spill disaster.

Senator Warren Henderson of Sarasota was fair to the fishing industry and supported fishermen throughout his illustrious career. He made every shrimping trip to Fort Jefferson. He was a master story teller and great minority leader.

Senators Verle Pope, Jack Mathews, Jerry Thomas and all the Senate presidents before the modern era, post 1983, gave the fishing industry access to their offices and helped keep them out of harm's way. When Jerry Thomas was Senate President he referred an anti-fishing bill to the committee on mental health. When the sponsor asked why he did that, Thomas told him the bill was crazy. The bill was never heard by any committee.

Senator Pat Thomas was a lot like Dempsey Barron. Thomas represented some of the most productive fishing areas in the state, especially Gulf and Franklin Counties. Thomas was one of the best friends the fishing industry ever had. He was smart, funny and a master politician who knew how to gain consensus on important issues. He was an old-school senator. If he gave you his word, he would not renege or change unless the person he gave his word to told him it was okay. Besides being a powerful leader in the legislative process, he was a fine human being whose bigger than life presence lit up a room.

Florida Senate Presidents from Dan McCarty in 1941 through Pat Thomas in 1994 were, for the most part, friends of the commercial fishermen. They allowed opportunities to fully examine anti-fishing legislation when they were in the chair. Curtis Peterson was president in 1983 when the Florida Marine Fisheries Commission was created, but looked to Senator Barron for guidance on all fisheries issues.

Florida Speakers of the House of Representatives like Bill Chappell, Mallory Horne, Don Tucker, Dick Pettigrew, James Harold Thompson, T.K. Wetherell, Fred Schultz, Terrell Sessums, Lee Moffitt, and Bolley Johnson, to name a few, were accessible and had a clear understanding about the importance of the industry and the importance of saving their culture.

The Florida seafood industry was regulated by the

legislature from 1913 until 1983 when authority was given to the Marine Fisheries Commission and the Florida Cabinet. Under legislative protocols, fishermen were given a fair hearing ninety-nine percent of the time. There was always a time and committee to fully explain their point of view during some juncture of the legislative process.

It was a sad day for democracy when the fishing industry was removed from regulation by elected officials. The 1998 constitutional amendments vested all authority over Florida fish and wildlife in the hands of seven gubernatorial appointees. There is no legislative oversight or administrative challenge allowed. Any disagreement must go to a court of competent jurisdiction where the state pays for the commission's lawyers, but fishermen must hire their own with meager funds. Adequate Due Process is lacking for the Florida fishing industry.

Several legislators were challenging to deal with during their term of office, but I will not mention them. There were only a few who got personal instead of sticking to the issue, but that is life. Under our form of government, legitimate differences of opinions must be debated before a legislative body. Where there is honest, open debate there is freedom. When honest debate is prohibited, everyone suffers.

Looking back from 1950 to 1980, most legislators had a warm spot for the fishing industry. They understood how hard commercial fishermen worked to provide fresh seafood. The legislators in those three decades were primarily Floridians, or people who had lived in Florida long enough to appreciate the seafood industry.

Around 1980, national politics became more partisan, intense and mean-spirited. The partisanship trickled down to Florida over the next three decades and is still trickling. The fishermen lost standing with elected officials representing all regions of the state. Fishermen do not have financial resources to participate in statewide campaigns or hire a cadre of lawyer-lobbyists. They cannot hobnob at galas or black-tie receptions because they are on the water in their boats trying to make a living.

The nation's fishing industry changed forever when anti-fishing groups gained control of policymaking at the state and federal levels.

CHAPTER 27

The Tarp Seine Baitfish Net

FOLLOWING THE 1995 FLORIDA NET BAN, THE SEVEN FISHING BOATS USING PURSE SEINES TO CATCH BAIT IN STATE WATERS DEVELOPED A UNIQUE NET MADE FROM TARPAULIN SO THEY COULD CONTINUE TO LEGALLY HARVEST BAITFISH INSHORE.

Gene Raffield and his brothers Harold, Ronnie, Danny and their dad Captain Carl discussed the possibility of creating a tarp net using 500 square feet of small mesh webbing which was legal.

At the same time, Dewey Destin in Destin, Florida, Jerry Melvin and the Barfield family in Panama City were using tarp nets in place of their historical purse seines to catch bait. They were making a living using the tarps. The baitfish fishermen, whose families had been fishermen for generations, were anxious to preserve their culture and way of life on the sea.

The baitfish companies were members of Southeastern Fisheries Association so they organized a Tarp Seine Section to lobby for state approval of the tarp nets. The Marine Patrol officers told the fishermen, when they boarded their boats for inspection, that the nets were legal because they contained less than 500 square feet of mesh. The harvest took twice as long and the poundage was 30% of a normal catch using purse seines, but the tarp nets produced much needed cigar minnows, menhaden, Spanish sardines, blue runners and ladyfish.

Gene Raffield and Dewey Destin led the fight for legislative approval of the tarp nets after their use was challenged by an angler lobbying organization. After numerous committee meetings, Senator Pat Thomas, Democrat from Quincy, who represented several counties where tarp nets were being used, brought Senator Jack Latvala, (R) Pinellas County, CCA's lobbyist, Dewey Destin and me into his office to hammer out a compromise. I think the fisheries commission's executive director, Ken Haddad, was also present.

As a result of the meeting, the fish commission agreed to conduct a three year scientific study on the tarp net baitfish fishery and report back to the legislature on the results.

In return for the three-year scientific pilot study, the tarp net fishermen agreed to support an amendment to the Florida statutes stipulating that in the future tarpaulin or any other material used as part of the net could be no greater than 500 square feet. The tarp net fishermen thought it was better to have a definition of a tarp net in statute instead of in the state constitution.

The trusting and completely naïve commercial fishermen thought they had a deal with the state and research would be undertaken to see whether or not a tarp net fishery harmed the resources in any manner. Little did they know the cards were already stacked against them. There was no intent by the state to conduct honest research. They deliberately stalled for the three years allowed by the legislature to conduct research then closed the tarp net fishery down.

When Dewey Destin and Senator Clary, (R) Republican from Destin, finally got an appropriation through the legislature to conduct the study, there was only a year left in the three year program and we didn't have the power to extend the research period. After the biologist assigned as observer on the tarp net boats reported no bycatch and no harm to the bottom, he was transferred. This was one time the state research program seemed manipulated to satisfy the militant anglers and a powerful senator who did not want fishermen on the water with any kind of net. The three years allowed by the legislature for a scientific evaluation ran out. The tarp net baitfish fishery was killed by the state.

Dewey Destin and I attended a Fish and Wildlife Commission meeting in Jacksonville to ask for approval of the tarp nets. When Dewey Destin and I saw a convicted felon who wanted to ban bait fishing in Florida so he could sell his imported baitfish from Central America, we knew something rotten was about to happen to the tarp fishermen. He had a big smile on his face. Unbeknownst to us or any fisherman, the convicted felon was allowed to testify the day before us even though the published agenda did not include that item.

The next day when Dewey Destin and I were given our three minutes each to save jobs and a baitfish industry, the decision by the commissioners had already been made. The Commission voted unanimously to ban tarp baitfish nets on purely political grounds. That action proved that the Fish and Wildlife Commission can ban any kind of fishing gear if four of the seven appointees vote together. It is a sad commentary on society when four non-elected gubernatorial appointees have such un-checked power. This is not a good system to live under.

The Panhandle baitfish companies were devastated by this decision and filed a lawsuit. In the final analysis, a few heads rolled at Fish and Wildlife but the tarp net ban prevailed, shutting down the use of a net with zero by-catch and the ability to release any and all fish alive.

CHAPTER 28

The shrimp industry's deep roots

THE SHRIMPING FAMILIES I KNEW IN ST. AUGUSTINE WERE MOST-
LY ITALIAN AND MOSTLY CATHOLIC. They were part of the
great immigration era at the beginning of the 20ᵗʰ century. Many of these new citizens settled in New York,
Fernandina and St. Augustine before moving on to Fort
Myers, Tampa, Louisiana, and Texas in pursuit of shrimp
from the Gulf of Mexico.

I attended St. Joseph's Academy High School with
Fazios, Tringali's, Tringle's, d'Augusta's and Militello's.
I knew the Poli's, Salvador's, Pacetti's, Lanasa's and
Versaggi's. I coached Darrell Poli when he played on the
Junior Varsity football team. His family has been a key
participant in the fishing industry for over one hundred
years, the same as so many other Italian families. The
Versaggi Corporation was formed in 1904 and is still ac-
tive in Tampa.

Joe Fazio was a high school classmate of mine and life
long friend. My brother Richard married Angie Militello,
the love of his life. During those carefree, youthful years
I had no idea I would spend nearly fifty years of my
life protecting the culture of commercial fishermen and
fighting for the survival of a very fragile food-producing
industry.

The Versaggi family arrived in America the same time as Solecito Salvador, whom I have written about in other chapters. John Versaggi was born in Sicily and was the oldest of the Versaggi brothers. He was the first Versaggi I ever met. That was in 1950. His father, Salvatore Versaggi, and Antonio Poli were Solecito Salvador's brothers-in-law.

John was a friend of my wife's family. He served in the state legislature for several years during the time my wife Malinda's father, F. Charles Usina, also served.

John was a big man with a giant handshake. He smiled every time I ever talked to him and was a pleasure to be around. After I went to work for Southeastern Fisheries Association, I became friends with his brothers, Manny and Virgil and nephews Sal and Joe who still work at their shrimp facility in Tampa. I met their father, Joe, a few years ago when we had a pleasant breakfast meeting at the Village Inn on Dale Mabry in Tampa.

Manny and his wife Pat were known for many good things. One of the most enjoyable was the cocktail hour and cookout in front of their house on St. Augustine Beach. This event happened every weekend they were in town. Manny loved to have his friends pull his beach seine to catch a few mullet, whiting and maybe a flounder every now and then. It was fun. Malinda and I enjoyed being part of their big family during summers at the Usina's beach cottage, especially eating the great fennel sausages he brought from Tampa to grill for his visitors and playing rousing card games.

If you participated in pulling the beach seine, Manny presented a signed and sealed certificate attesting your graduation from the Sam Houston Institute of Technology as a bonafide seine fishermen. This wonderful pastime was banned when pier fishermen got a law passed that stopped seine fishermen from doing something that had no adverse impact on fish.

Northeast Florida produced shrimp leaders with a passion to improve and expand the fledgling Florida fishing industry after World War II. Fernandina's Sloan and Bluff Peterson, David Cook, Tony Tringali, Y.E. Hall, Billy Burbank, the Litrico's and many other families worked together for the good of everyone.

Mayport's Pack family is still active in all phases of the seafood industry and is one of the largest shrimp packers/processors on the east coast. Few shrimp houses are still actively unloading fishing boats because of all the state and federal regulations. Gerald Pack's upscale, immaculately clean restaurant/retail market serves one of the best grouper sandwiches in the country.

The Mat Roland and G.A. Leek families were stalwarts during the shrimping heyday and were prosperous businesses until normalization with China and Vietnam began. Roland was among the many Portuguese men who became shrimpers after arriving in America. Captain John Carinhas Santos played a pivotal role in moving the shrimp industry forward.

Jake Flowers is the last man standing in Fernandina, operating a modern shrimp processing facility and doing everything he can to compete with pond-raised shrimp from overseas that make up ninety percent of US shrimp consumption.

Fernandina was the final stronghold for menhaden processing at a plant owned and operated by the Exteen Corbett family. Florida demographics changed and so did the historical essence of the state. New residents to Fernandina, a place where seafood harvesters were respected for decades, opposed "Porgy-plants" and working waterfronts. Men in commercial fishing boats are prevented from fishing near gated-communities and golf courses built on filled-in marshes and wetlands.

The Hardee families were invaluable to the U.S. fishing industry. Without the suppliers who sold nets, boats and gear the fishing industry would never have progressed. Baker, Jimmy, Bill and David Hardee and all allied businesses worked hard back then to supply the needs of the fishermen. It is difficult watching globalization decimate so many seafood businesses that have operated for generations.

CHAPTER 29

One of a kind

I HAVE BEEN TOLD THERE WAS A LARGE PORTRAIT IN A GOLDEN FRAME ON THE WALL BEHIND A CASHIER'S CAGE AT A FAMOUS LAS VEGAS CASINO. The distinguished looking man with gray hair and expensive suit had a smile on his face. The bronze plate at the bottom of the frame said, "The Roving Gambler."

I wager not any person who has seen that portrait could ever imagine the man in the portrait started his fishing career on a shrimp dock and working a mullet skiff in Mayport, Florida. I believe the "Roving Gambler" was in grade school with my mother when her family, the Brinson's, lived in Mayport. She once told me that she had a crush on a boy in her class by the name of Henry Singleton. It is weird and wonderful how people move in and out of each other's lives.

By the time I met Henry C. Singleton he was known as "Booty" Singleton by everyone in the shrimp business. The year was 1965. He was well established as a man who personified the American Dream. He owned dozens of shrimp boats, several unloading docks and a modern shrimp processing plant on 50th Street in Tampa.

I called on Booty at his plush office during one of my first trips to Tampa and was treated kindly. One of his production managers gave me my first tour of a modern shrimp processing plant. I had never seen so many shrimp or so many people working so hard, in harmony. I was grossly uninformed on the intricacies and nuances of the shrimp industry.

After the grand tour I returned to Booty's office. As always, I told him I had a lot to learn and was willing to listen. I was contented knowing the Board of Directors had written policies for me to conduct my activities and there was a cadre of members willing and ready to help me at all times.

I told Booty about the progress Jack Brawner, Harmon Shields and I were making with the coopera- tive seafood marketing program, but he was not very enthusiastic about our marketing program. He preferred individual seafood companies doing their own marketing. I shrugged and changed the subject to the association's main project which was establishing a nursery area for pink shrimp in the Tortugas.

The moment I mentioned the subject of pink shrimp I realized I should have raised another subject. His friendly attitude vanished. His demeanor toughened and I re- ceived my first lecture on why the association should not be involved in setting the size of shrimp to be harvested. My face flushed. I was being intimidated for following association policy to protect the pink shrimp resource. After he finished, I had nothing else to say but I was get- ting angry. He made his position known to me quite well so I was ready to leave. I listened but had no intention of changing what the board told me to do.

We shook hands. I told him thanks for the tour of his

processing plant. I didn't realize it then but my honeymoon with the association ended in Booty's office. The war to protect Florida juvenile pink shrimp was on. Booty Singleton and I would be on opposite sides of the conservation issue for years.

I met with shrimpers in Fort Myers and Key West after I left Tampa and told them about my experience with Booty. They said not to worry about him. They would handle him if he complained again and would tell him I was doing my job so let me be. My first meeting with Booty taught me that as long as I upheld the policies of the association, I would never have to worry about losing my job.

There was no need to talk to Booty again about the pink shrimp nursery area. I did not talk to him again for almost a year until I was on my way to the Tallahassee General Aviation airport to join legislators going to Fort Jefferson to learn how we catch pink shrimp and why baby shrimp need protection.

When I walked into the waiting room at the airport Harmon Shields came over and told me he had received a call from his office that my secretary, Newell Croy, got a call from Mr. Singleton. She said he wanted me to call him before I got on the airplane. I did not have much time, but I went into the lounge and called from a pay phone.

"What can I do for you, Mr. Singleton?" I said, after his secretary got him on the line.

"Do not go to Key West on the shrimping trip," he

said in a not too friendly manner.

"I am leaving in a few minutes. I am in charge of getting our guests down there," I responded. "What is the problem?"

"I pay a lot of money to Southeastern Fisheries and if you go on this trip I will pull my money out and form another association," he said.

"Do what you have to do, Mr. Singleton. I am leaving now," I said in a low voice, but with much anger in my heart.

I was already loaded down with responsibility to get everyone on time to the Key West dock. I did not appreciate the added pressure he placed on me. I hung up the phone, looked at the ground for a second or so, then walked quickly to Harmon Shields' waiting plane. The door was open and the engine running. I climbed into the co-pilot seat of the Cessna 172 and headed for the Key West International Airport.

True to his word, Booty and his good friend Bob Wilson formed the Florida Shrimp Association and opened an office in Tampa. It remained our opposition for several years until the shrimp nursery area was established. Then, after numerous joint meetings with leaders of Southeastern Fisheries Association, they rejoined.

Booty remained an active member of the association until his death and our relationship was cordial. I only had the chance to work with one of his children, a man who has spent his adult life helping others. Mark Singleton believes in helping the "least of the brothers." I think his daddy would have been proud of Mark and his good works.

CHAPTER 30

Beaver Street Fisheries Mr. Harry

FISH BUSINESS ON WEST BEAVER STREET BEGAN IN EARNEST FOL-
LOWING WORLD WAR II WHEN RATIONING ENDED AND CONSUMER
GOODS WERE ONCE AGAIN AVAILABLE ON THE OPEN MARKET, IN-
STEAD OF JUST THE BLACK MARKET. New jobs and myriad
businesses were created all over Florida, especially in
Jacksonville. Harry Frisch was a fishery pioneer who
helped Jacksonville grow and prosper. These are a few
words about him.

Harry joined his mother, step-father and brother Alfred
in the fish market his mother owned on Beaver Street.
It was 1955 and Harry was working as an automobile
mechanic and doing very well. He was the go to guy
for Western Auto for replacing car engines. Before Harry
took over Western Auto's engine replacement program it
had a 67% return rate on engines they installed. When
he was in charge, and until the day he left, they had a
zero percentage return for Western Auto rebuilt engines
installed by Harry Frisch. He demanded perfection from
the mechanics who worked under his tutelage.

The family built Beaver Street Fisheries from a very
small venture, buying fish wherever they could, then selling them to a growing customer base in the Northeast
Florida market. Harry remembers getting to work at 5:00

AM, driving to fish docks to pick up whiting, flounder, crab and shrimp, then bringing the fish back to Beaver Street for cleaning and packing, hoping that Alfred had been on the phone long enough to sell what they had bought that day.

My daddy was an automobile mechanic in Southside Jacksonville and was partner at the Koenig and Jones Service Station on the corner of San Marco Boulevard and LaSalle Street. He might have known Harry because he fixed a lot of cars for fish folks in West Jacksonville. They had one thing in common - they both knew the day would come when they would not be able to get off the creeper they used to check underneath cars. Harry was smart and left the creepers in 1955 at the age of thirty, but my daddy stayed under the cars until he was in his early eighties.

Harry told me his auto mechanic abilities came in handy during the early days of Beaver Street Fisheries. He had to fix some of the trucks every weekend so they could deliver fish on Monday. Without his ability with tools the company could not deliver fresh fish.

I met Harry Frisch in 1964. By then his business was growing by leaps and bounds. My main contact then was Harry Salisbury Jr. a world-class fish peddler and astute businessman. He spent his career working for Harry and was active in all aspects of fisheries matters for several decades. Darrell Glover, Peter Newton and George Farah are the go-to guys who are carrying on the tradition of honest weight and fair price.

Harry has a quality control program that checks every purchase to make sure it meets his strict specifications.

BEAVER STREET FISHERIES MR. HARRY

I was in his office one day while he was checking the weight on a certain farm-raised fish commodity. "Bob," he said as he scrolled down his computer looking the actual weight on the item. "You know, some of these people selling me farmed catfish think thirteen ounces is a pound."

"How do you handle that, Harry?" I asked.

"Simple, I cut the ticket, show them the net weight we received and pay them the corrected invoice based on real weight," he smiled. "They don't even question our system anymore because they know we are right."

Beaver Street is one of the largest seafood companies in the southeast. They have been recognized by many groups for their generosity to many segments of the Jacksonville community. A photograph in their reception room shows Harry dressed in a Jacksonville Jaguar uniform, looking like a fleet-footed tailback or middle linebacker.

Harry has a plant in Miami and built a modern spiny lobster factory in the Bahamas years ago to be close to the source. It is a state-of-the art facility. His brand is known throughout the world.

There are not too many pioneers like Harry Frisch still working five, sometimes six days a week. At 88 years young he knows what is going on, in detail, anywhere in his big plant located at the foot of the bridge across from the Farmer's Market on Beaver Street. Harry said he has had a wonderful life because he has a wonderful wife. That, Mr. Harry, is something the entire fishing agrees on. Everyone knows getting the fishing industry to agree on anything is rare.

CHAPTER 31

A crystal ball statement
by Gene Raffield written in June 1976

WHEN CLYDE KITCHEL TOLD ME THAT SERVING AS PRESIDENT OF SOUTHEASTERN FISHERIES ASSOCIATION WOULD BE REWARDING, BUT VERY BUSY, HE WAS TELLING IT LIKE IT IS. No sooner had I taken office when the traveling began. Trips to Washington seemed to come about every two weeks. Conferences in Tallahassee, St. Petersburg and regular Area Meetings kept me on the road at least once a month.

In August our spiny lobster members were booted out of the Bahamas because of the Magnuson Stevens Act. Bob Jones had to fly to Nassau for two weeks as an advisor to the U.S. State Department. They tried to craft an agreement but were unsuccessful. We got close once, but we found out our issue had to take the back seat to "broader national interests." Maybe we can persuade the Bahamian Government to reopen negotiations or we try to have the Bensten amendment invoked. Senator Bensten's amendment would prohibit the importation of Bahamian-caught spiny lobsters until good faith negotiations began. Scuttlebutt at the time was U.S. submarines needed anchorage at the Tongue of the Ocean on the east side of the island.

A CULTURE WORTH SAVING

Regardless of the politics, Southeastern Fisheries Association pushed for national spiny lobster legislation and testified before several Congressional committees. However, the National Fisheries Institute had reservations concerning the legislation and were able to stop any progress. At this writing, we are waiting for the opponents to offer amendments to satisfy their objections.

We worked diligently to defeat of the 200-mile bill but were unsuccessful. We knew our distant water shrimp, spiny lobster and reef fish fleets would be harmed by the passage of the 200-mile bill.

In the summer we hosted our annual fishing trip to the Dry Tortugas for the leaders of the Florida Legislature. It was, as usual, a very successful outing. The legislators who attended all caught lots of fish and had a great time catching and heading shrimp on the trip to the Fort. They learned a great deal about the commercial fishing industry and that is what this legislative trip is all about. Without the untiring cooperation of our Key West members, especially Pete and Jeanette Toomer, Edwin and Marci Felton and John and Nora Koenig, this trip would not be possible. We thank them very much for all they do for the industry.

I attended a National Policy Conference Meeting in Washington where most of the regional and national fisheries associations were present. We discussed issues affecting the US commercial fishing industry and passed some important resolutions concerning financial assistance, marketing, utilization and technical assistance. I observed how well respected our Association has become in the past ten years. I wish every member had an opportunity to participate in the programs that I have this year. I guarantee if each member did we would have a lot more of them asking others in the industry to join.

We continue trying to get Florida's education system to include commercial fishing in their core curriculum. There are a few seafood industry related courses taught at the junior college level that help, indirectly, but not the kind of programs needed to upgrade the industry.

Education Commissioner Ralph Turlington is receptive to plugging us in if we can find the right curriculum, place and time. This is a far-reaching program that must be continued.

In my travels this year there was a great amount of enthusiasm. Even with all the problems we have had on fuel prices, and increased costs at every turn, members of the industry are optimistic about the future. I guess this is what keeps us in the fishing industry, hoping that we will make the big catch on the next trip.

The investigation by the U.S. Justice Department on price fixing has caused a lot of discussion in and out of the industry. We just received a copy of the letter to the Justice Department from Senators Johnston of Louisiana and Hollings of South Carolina calling for this investigation back in 1974.

When the association was contacted by the U.S. Justice Department, Bob Jones personally delivered all association financial records to Atlanta. He left them with the Justice Department for their perusal under the subpoena that was issued to the association. Bob said the officials at the Justice Department office seemed surprised when he walked in with a cardboard box of audits and voluntary shrimp contribution records and asked them if they had any questions. They said they did not.

As of today, no further communication has come from the Justice Department. I can reassure each and every member of Southeastern Fisheries Association that your Association never has, nor ever will, engage in any kind of price fixing.

Our Workmen's Compensation Program and group Health Insurance Program continue to grow. We have thirty five members in our Workmen's Comp Program generating a premium over $250,000. We were able to return $20,000 to the participating members last year and hope to do as well this year.

Our Semi-Annual meeting was held in Key West and what a great time everyone had. It had been seventeen years since we held a meeting in Key West. The local members put on a Board meeting that was the best in recent memory.

During the early part of this year, the Association officers learned how the Federal budget process worked. We attended several sessions with various government agencies and understand the system a little better, but not as well as we need to. We learned enough to give Bob Jones confidence to testify before the House Appropriations Committee. Hopefully, we will be able to testify each year from now on. Testifying to a congressional committee is the only way our views are articulated to Congress.

A CRYSTAL BALL STATEMENT

One of the most serious problems that could develop within the next year is mandatory protection of sea turtles. Southeastern Fisheries Association and Texas Shrimp Association are very involved in developing rules and regulations that will impact the entire shrimping fleet from North Carolina to Texas. We must be willing to modify the gear and methods we have used in the past in protecting turtles that now are on the threatened and endangered species list. We might be called on to help, financially, in rearing turtles in hatcheries to replace any turtles accidentally drowned in our nets.

We must launch an intensive education campaign within the industry letting fishermen know just how strong the Endangered Species Act Legislation is in the United States. If we don't offer protection suitable for maintaining and increasing the turtle stock, the Federal Government will adopt rules that greatly reduce our ability to produce seafood. If the Endangered Species Act was strong enough to shut down the tuna fishery, it is strong enough to shut down the shrimp fishery or any segment of the commercial fishing industry.

There are many programs your Association works on for your behalf. Being intimately involved in all of them this past year has increased my support for Southeastern. The Association has handled several hundred different matters for individual members this year as they do every year, from unemployment compensation to sales tax problems to proposed net bans and other kinds of limitations.

The last few months have been spent in preparation

for the Florida legislature, Congressional testimony, this Convention and U.S.-Mexican talks on continued shrimping within Mexico's 200-mile economic zone.

I suppose there have been other years that have been busier and more complex than this year, but I'm glad this year was mine.

I thank you for giving me this privilege. I pledge my full support to President-elect Paul Herring during the coming year. My heartfelt thanks go to Bob Jones, Newell Lee, Eleanor Strawbridge and Malinda Jones for doing more work on behalf of the commercial fishing industry than anyone will ever realize.

CHAPTER 32

The hiring of Bob Jones

MY LATE FATHER-IN-LAW, STATE REP. F. CHARLES USINA OF ST. AUGUSTINE, FLORIDA CALLED ME IN MAY OF 1964 AND ASKED IF I WANTED TO APPLY FOR A JOB IN TALLAHASSEE WORKING AS THE EXECUTIVE SECRETARY OF SOUTHEASTERN FISHERIES ASSOCIATION. He said the decision would be made in a couple of weeks during the association's 12th annual convention.

I was living in Houston, Texas with my wife Mindy, Usina's oldest daughter, and our four children, managing a motel and restaurant on Katy Highway. I had recently finished serving as the manager of internal affairs of the U.S. Jaycees on the national staff in Tulsa. Making ends meet, even working seven days a week, was a monthly struggle so a chance for a better job and going home to Florida loomed large in my world. I was thirty years old and still maintained the weight carried when honorably discharged from the Marine Corps nine years earlier.

"I'd love to apply for the job as executive director of a trade association," I told Mr. Usina.

"You'll be interviewed in Miami Beach and I'll send an airplane ticket," he quickly offered.

"Thanks, I said as I handed the phone to Malinda who was very excited about the possibility of moving back to Florida.

Before I knew it I was landing at the Miami International Airport. Then I was riding in a Yellow cab headed to Miami Beach. When I arrived at the Carillon Hotel and walked into the lobby it looked like a movie set. There were polished marble columns holding up high ceilings, plush carpets that felt like they came up to my ankles, enormous couches where five or six large people could sit all at once, glass-top coffee tables and dozens of multicolored fabric chairs in the huge lobby. I had never been in a Miami Beach hotel before and was in awe at the richness.

After checking in the uniformed bellman carried my well-worn Samsonite piece of luggage—packed with a clean shirt, my only other tie, underwear and toiletries—to a marvelous room overlooking the waves breaking on snow white sand. I tipped the friendly bellman two dollars which was a lot of money back then, especially for me.

I soaked in the view; the king-size bed with a dozen pillows and brocade headboard and two overstuffed chairs at each end of the thick glass and brass coffee table. The message light on the bedside phone was blinking. The operator asked me to call Johnny Salvador as soon as I arrived to receive instructions for my interview. Johnny told me there were three people on the interview team: Ralph Aylesworth of St. Petersburg, who was a pioneer in the Florida fish business, Y.E. Hall, an insurance company owner in Fernandina who also owned several shrimp boats, and Bob Young, who owned a successful crab-packing plant in downtown Fernandina.

THE HIRING OF BOB JONES

I don't remember many of the questions asked by the interviewers but I do remember that the three men were very friendly and I felt the interview went well. I told them I looked forward to the board meeting the following morning when an executive director would be selected. They had several other candidates to interview including a member of the Florida House of Representatives and a prominent marine scientist from the University of Miami, although I didn't know that at the time.

After the interview I was given a copy of the Convention Booklet. Governor Carl Sanders of Georgia was the guest speaker at the Saturday night banquet. Mayor Hayden Burns of Jacksonville, who would become Governor, was a speaker at the general session as well as H.E. "Skip" Crowther, head of the U.S. Bureau of Commercial Fisheries. I didn't know any of these gentlemen at the time, but it was obvious Southeastern Fisheries Association was respected by fishery and political leaders in the southeast as well as Washington, D.C.

When it came time for the Board of Directors meeting, I was nervous. I didn't know anyone but Johnny Salvador, co-owner of Salvador's Seafood Company in St. Augustine and Tony Meitin, Vice President of the St. Augustine National Bank. Salvador was the Chairman and Meitin was Treasurer. I knew there would be two-friendly-faces among the twenty-five members of the board.

When I entered the room I recognized Ralph Aylesworth, Y.E. Hall and Bob Young. They interviewed me and were on the board which made me feel a bit more comfortable.

I explained growing up in St. Augustine and winning the state award for having the best Jaycee Club in Florida when I was President of the St. Augustine Jaycees. I further explained how that experience led to working on the Jaycees national staff in Tulsa, Oklahoma. I emphasized my Jaycee duties included increasing membership, membership retention, teaching Robert's Rules of Order, writing news articles and coordinating national projects.

I said I was honorably discharged from the USMC. I talked about working on an offshore shrimp boat with Capt. Raymond Sykes, a one-armed World War II veteran. Besides ocean shrimping I explained how I worked at P.J. Manucy's Riverside Fish Camp catching bait shrimp with Conch Edge, an old and respected river fisherman known to many fishermen in the region. The interview was moving in a friendly fashion when something caught my eye.

Directly across from me sat a big crusty-looking man with white, wavy-hair wearing horn-rimmed glasses. He had a massive cigar in his mouth. He wasn't smoking, just chewing and rolling it around on his tongue and listening intently to every word I spoke. He had a twinkle in his eye I thought was menacing, not friendly.

When I finished my remarks and the room became quiet, he leaned forward in his chair, looked me square in the eyes and said, "Mr. Jones, are you too good to walk on a dock, sit on a fish box, and talk to fishermen?"

I looked straight back into the eyes of this intense man. I felt my face flush. I didn't know him and didn't like being asked if I was too good to do anything. I started to respond in the same hard tone he used, but before any words left my mouth, Johnny Salvador said in a strong voice, "Mr. Rice, Mr. Jones was a bricklayer for five years, and he's not afraid to get his hands dirty."

The board meeting went silent for what seemed like ten minutes, but was probably thirty seconds. Mr. Rice took the giant Cuban cigar out of his mouth with his left hand, slammed his massive right hand on the polished mahogany table, and said in a booming voice, "By God, I move we hire the boy." I was stunned. The interview ended.

I waited outside the meeting room while they made their decision, then was called in and told I was selected for the position of Executive Secretary of the Southeastern Fisheries Association. The smile on my face must have been from ear to ear because all around the table everyone was smiling back. Well, almost everyone. I thanked them and pledged to do the best job possible.

The Chairman told me to report for work in Tallahassee on August 1, 1984. They voted to pay me $7,500 a year, provide a company car and consider other benefits as soon as they could afford them. I was on cloud nine by winning a steady job, a biweekly paycheck and coming home to Florida.

I found later out that C.C. "Charlie" Rice, the man with the big cigar and large presence, was a master politician with friends throughout the country. He owned successful fish businesses in Pinellas County and Honduras where he dealt easily with all kinds of politicians including the dictator of Honduras.

A CULTURE WORTH SAVING

Mr. Charlie, as most people called him, turned out to be a strong mentor and shared stories of his young adulthood in Danville, Illinois that were riveting and sometimes frightening.

My interview at the Carillon Hotel on Miami Beach was a life-changing event leading me down the path of a modern-era gunslinger for the commercial fishing industry. I cherish the memory of those few sweet moments facing the board of directors and the opportunities they gave me the past five decades.

I've thought back to that day in Miami Beach and felt I must have cut a fine figure during the interview. I must have been extremely articulate to win the job over several candidates who I thought were more qualified. Then one day driving home from a meeting in South Florida I figured out what really happened.

I was the son-in-law of a member of the Legislature who championed issues for the deaf and blind and for all working people, including commercial fishermen. The Chairman of Southeastern Fisheries Association, Johnny Salvador, and the Treasurer Tony Meitin, were both from St. Augustine as was Past President L.C. Ringhaver. These men were all close friends of Charlie Usina, my wonderful father-in-law. I am totally convinced they lobbied the board members on my behalf without a word being said by any of them to me. There was no way I could fail the interview because those who wanted me had the votes.

I'm thankful my naivety let me believe for twenty-five years it was my skillful remarks and good looks that

THE HIRING OF BOB JONES

got me the job with Southeastern Fisheries Association. That's not what happened. But, while it wasn't my skills that got me hired, it was my skills and the blessings of God that have kept me working in the same job for the same association for nearly fifty years. I didn't recognize at the time what those good men did for me and my family. I do now. I carry a warm place in my heart for the men who knew and loved Charlie Usina enough to hire his son-in-law and allow him to dedicate his career to a culture worth saving.

CPSIA information can be obtained at www.ICGtesting.com
Printed in the USA
LVOW12s0528100714

393711LV00001B/1/P